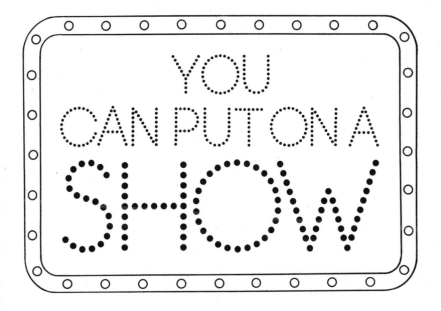

YOU CAN PUT ON A SHOW

BY LEWY OLFSON

Illustrations by
Shizu Matsuda and Santa De Haven

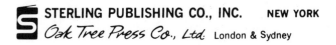

STERLING PUBLISHING CO., INC.   NEW YORK
Oak Tree Press Co., Ltd. London & Sydney

BY THE SAME AUTHOR
You Can Act!

IN THE SAME FIELD

Best Singing Games for Children

Carpentry for Children

Costumes from Crepe Paper

Dancing Games for Children of All Ages

Hokus Pokus

Humorous Monologues

Masks

Monster Masks

Movement Games

101 Best Magic Tricks

Pantomimes, Charades, Skits

Postercraft

Puppet and Pantomime Plays

Puppet-Making

Dedication

For
Pauline Winnick
after more than twenty years of friendship

DS

792·0226

Contents

Why Put On a Show?

There are lots of reasons.

You can put on a show to have something to do. It takes a lot of time and it takes a lot of work. Putting on a show is a good way for you and your friends to keep busy and to pass the time when there isn't a lot going on.

You can put on a show to entertain people. Perhaps the parents of the girls and boys in your class are going to come to school one evening. Putting on a show with your classmates would be a good way to entertain them. Or, there may be an assembly at school for which you would like to provide entertainment. Perhaps you would like to entertain a group of patients at a children's hospital, or the people who live in a home for elderly folks. Maybe there's a jamboree of Scout groups coming up, or maybe the families that belong to your church are planning a big get-together. Any time and any place that a group of people gather could be a reason for putting on a show.

You can put on a show to raise money. Perhaps you and your friends want to make a contribution to some important charity. Or perhaps your club needs to raise some money for its treasury. Or maybe you and your friends just want to make a little extra spending money. As long as you don't expect to raise a great deal of money, but just a small amount, a show that you put on can be the perfect answer.

But the *best* reason to put on a show is—just for the fun of it!

Even though there's a lot of hard work involved in putting on a show, there is also a lot of fun in such a project. You have fun getting ready for the show. You have fun doing the show itself. And you have fun afterwards, when everyone tells you what a terrific job you did, and what a great show it was.

So, if you have an important reason to put on a show, do it, but if you *don't* have an important reason to put on a show—do it anyway! Just for the fun of it! Just because you want to!

1. What Kind of Show Will It Be?

The first step is to decide just what kind of show to put on. Will it be a variety show? A one-act play? A puppet show? A revue? A pageant? A recital? Some other kind of show?

This is an important decision. You and your friends should talk it over carefully among yourselves. You're going to be putting in a lot of time on your show, and you're going to be working hard on it. You want to be sure that everyone involved agrees on the kind of show it is to be.

Some of the things you will have to consider in making your decision are the following:

How many kids are going to be involved? If lots of boys and girls are to work on the show—a whole class, say, or a whole Scout troop—you can plan a lengthy show with lots of people in it. If just a few of you are to do the show, on the other hand, you will want to choose one of the simpler kinds of shows. One person can even put on a show all by himself—a puppet show! No matter how many or how few kids there are, you can put on some kind of show. But you need to *know* how many there will be, so you can do a show big enough for everyone to work on it, yet have everyone do the job well.

Of course, not everyone who works on a show has to act in it. There are many jobs that need doing backstage as well as onstage. Depending on the kind of show you choose, you may need people to paint scenery, to make costumes, to run sound effects. You may need somebody to make signs and posters. You may need people to sell tickets. You may need people to serve refreshments. There are lots of jobs in putting on a show. So, in counting up the number of workers you will have, think of all the jobs involved, and not of just the performers. In Chapter 2 of this book, the different jobs are described in detail.

What are the talents of the people involved? Once you find out who is going to be working on the show, you need to know what those people do well. If you have nobody in your group who plays a musical instrument, for instance, you won't want to choose a show that needs live music. If there are six kids in your group who take dancing lessons and who want a chance to dance for an audience, you will want to choose a show with some dancing. If you have a good magician in your group, you'll surely want to put on a show that will call for magic tricks.

And what do the people want to do? You may have enough boys and girls to put on a play with ten parts in it, but do the boys and girls *want* to take parts in a play? They may not feel like memorizing lines (learning the words of their parts). They may not want to spend time rehearsing (practicing) together. By the same token, be sure there are people who want to design and build and paint scenery before you choose a show that needs scenery. Be sure you have people who like to work on arts and crafts projects before you choose a show that needs lots of new puppets.

And don't take it for granted that each person will be willing to take a job he or she is good at. Tom may be a whiz at playing the piano—but he may be sick of always playing the piano; he may want a chance to do something else. Just because Nancy gets all A's in art, it isn't fair just to assume that she will want to paint posters. Maybe this time she wants to try being an actress.

Where is the show going to be held? The place has to be considered before you can make a final decision about what kind of show to put on. There may be a problem or two. For instance, if you're going to do the show in somebody's back yard, you'd better accept the fact that your show will not have a piano. If your show is going to be given at the front of your classroom, there may not be enough room to plan a big dance number for, say, 16 dancers. If the show is going to be given in somebody's garage, you'll want to make sure you can use any electrical equipment you may need. If the show is going to be given in somebody's cellar, the puppet theatre you have in mind may be too large to get down the stairs.

Related to this is the matter of getting permission. Be sure that whatever teachers or parents need to give permission to use a certain place for putting on a show *are* asked—before you make your plans.

Who will the show be for? In deciding on the kind of show, it might be a good idea to think a bit about the audience you hope to have. What kind of show would

such an audience enjoy? If you're going to put on a show for the kindergarten children in your school, for example, you will need to plan a show that is short enough and lively enough to hold their interest. A show for a group of people at a retirement home should be planned with *that* audience in mind—don't do a show requiring electric guitars and loud rock music for them! If you're planning your show for an audience of parents, though, you're in luck. Parents can be counted on to enjoy any kind of show you put on!

In thinking about questions like these, plan to put on the kind of show that will really be the best choice for your group, and try to be realistic. It's natural to want to tackle a really big undertaking. And especially during the first planning stage, everyone will be most enthusiastic and eager to help. But it often happens that some people lose interest in the project somewhere along the way. As time goes on, there may be more and more work to do—and fewer and fewer people to do it. So, as a general rule, it's better to choose a show that is on the simple, uncomplicated side—especially if it is the first show you have ever put on. Later, when you have had some experience, you'll be in a better position to know just how elaborate and ambitious a project your friends and you can handle.

When you know pretty well how many you will have to work with, and what you can expect in the way of talent and energy and available space, you can decide on the best kind of show to give. Here are brief descriptions of the different possibilities. (Each of them will be discussed in more detail later on.)

The Variety Show

A variety show is about the least complicated kind of show there is. It consists of several different performers, each of whom does a short entertaining performance. The greater the difference between one "act" in a variety show and the next, the more enjoyable the show is likely to be. One variety show might be made up of the following: an accordionist, a comedian telling jokes, a folk dance, a singer, a magician, and a tap dance routine.

There are several advantages in putting on a variety show. Usually everyone who wants to perform gets a chance to do something as part of the show. The show can be as long or as short as you choose to make it. You don't need any special scenery, and if anyone needs a special costume, the chances are that he or she already owns the costume needed.

The one drawback to a variety show is that it really does need *variety*. If most of the performers in your group do the same kind of thing—if you have six people who want to sing, or four people who all do magic acts, or nine accordion players—the show will be too much one kind of entertainment. It's boring for an audience to see one after another performer putting on the same kind of performance. If, however, you can get all your singers to join and sing a couple of songs as a group, and you can persuade your magicians to work out a set of tricks that they can do together, and you can talk your accordionists into doing two or three group numbers, your problem is solved!

The Revue

A revue is like a variety show, in that it is made up of a number of individual acts. The difference, however, is that some of the acts are in the form of very short plays. In a revue there are even things called "running gags" and "blackout sketches" that may involve just a few spoken words. A revue has all the advantages of a variety show, with the added advantage that there are parts for boys and girls who don't do any special performing act (such as playing an instrument or dancing or singing or doing magic tricks), but who want to be in the show anyway.

Another advantage of the revue is that it can be given a theme. With a theme, all or most of the individual acts have something in common with one another. A revue with a Christmas theme, for example, would have something Christmas-y as part of each separate act. A revue with a theme of "Pioneer Days" would, similarly, have each act relate somehow to the subject of pioneers. This makes a revue an especially good choice when you want your show to tie in with something else that is going on—a holiday, a community celebration, a school event. Using a theme makes all of the separate acts "hang together," and makes the show seem "all of a piece," even though it is, in fact, several different, separate acts.

The One-Act Play

A play is a story acted out by several people. It is a good choice for a group in which the individual boys and girls don't have special performing skills.

There are several advantages to choosing a play.

One is that you can put on a play as simply or as elaborately as you like, depending on the number and talents of the people available. Your play can have just a few parts in it, or parts for dozens of actors. You can put on a play with no scenery at all, or you can put on one with several different fancy settings. The same goes for costumes. You can choose a play of whatever type you like: a wild, slapstick comedy, or spooky mystery, or magical make-believe.

If you want, putting on a play can give you special opportunities to be creative—to really use your imagination and brains. For example, you and your friends can write the play yourselves. Or you can put on a play in which you make up the lines as you go along.

But, in putting on a play, there are some problems that you should think about, too, before deciding. In a play, all the actors work with one another, so you must get together frequently as a group to practice. (In a variety show or a revue, the acts are separate from one another, so group rehearsals aren't a problem.) Unless you make up the lines as you go along, a play means having to memorize lines. That takes some study, and many kids just don't enjoy that part of being in a play. Also, a play needs a director—a boss—for every step of the way. (Variety shows and revues need a director, too, but the director of those shows just keeps things generally under control. The director of a play has a much more difficult task.) Are the kids in your group willing to follow the directions given them, or does everyone like being able to do things his or her own way? That's an important question to answer.

It may also take more time to get a play ready than

a variety show. The people who perform in a variety show already know how to do "their thing." The violinist has already learned his piece; the dancers already know how to dance; the magician has performed his magic act many times. You can put all these performers together for a variety show with a very small amount of rehearsal time. But for a play, everyone has to start from scratch. It's entirely a group effort, and requires the group to work together for a fair amount of time. So this becomes another consideration to keep in mind before settling definitely on this kind of show.

The Puppet Show

What do you do when everyone wants to put on a show, but nobody wants to actually be *in* a show in front of an audience? You put on a puppet show! That way, nobody has to worry about getting nervous about being looked at.

A puppet show is also a good choice when there are only a few boys and girls who want to put on a show, especially if those boys and girls are good at arts and crafts.

A puppet show has many of the same advantages and disadvantages of a one-act play. But in a puppet show, nobody has to learn any lines. Because the speakers are hidden from the audience, they get to read their lines from a book—and nobody in the audience is any the wiser!

Other Kinds of Shows

Some of the other kinds of shows you can give are the following:

A Pageant

This is a special show in which lots of people usually take small parts, and just a few people take big parts. In a pageant, there is usually a narrator, or story-teller, who stands at one side of the play area and tells the audience what is going on. The actors then perform short scenes, either in pantomime or with dialogue, to illustrate the story the narrator is telling. ("Pantomime" means acting without words; "dialogue" means words and lines spoken by actors.) A pageant usually tells the history of something—"Columbus and the New World," for example, or "Great Inventions of the Ages," or "Man's Conquest of Space." Pageants usually feature interesting things to look at—beautiful costumes, large groups of people moving in interesting ways, special scenery effects. Pageants tend to be very grand and elaborate, and are best put on by highly organized groups with adult leadership and some money in the treasury.

A Recital

A recital is a variety show in which all the performers put on the same sort of act. In a dance recital, each act is a different dance. In a piano recital, each act has a different performer playing the piano. In an elocution recital, each act has a different performer giving a recitation. And so on. Recitals are a good kind of show to put on when most of the boys and girls in your group have the same kind of talent or skill. They require no special costumes or scenery, which makes them easy to put on, but for most audiences they are not as entertaining as other kinds of shows.

A Performance Contest

When a number of kids are interested in being *in* a show, but very few of them are interested in *putting on* a show—in actually doing the planning and organizing that a show needs—a contest can be a good choice. The performers just show up at the appointed place at the right time, and "do their own thing" for the audience. A set of judges, or the whole audience, then decides whose performance was best, and that person is named the winner. It's that simple.

You can have an amateur talent contest, in which each performer puts on some sort of variety act: singing, magic, dancing, playing an instrument. Or you can have a contest to pick the "Blue Ribbon Kid" of your block, vicinity, or school.

For a "Blue Ribbon Kid" contest, you need a panel of judges, a big blue ribbon to give as a prize, and a bunch of kids to try for the prize. The contest can be in three parts. In the first part, each kid reads a short composition he has written on an assigned topic. (Some topics might be "Why I Like My Town," "Being a Good Citizen," "What I Would Do if I Were Mayor." Note that you only pick one topic for the contest, though. Every kid in the contest writes a composition on the same topic.) In the second part of the contest, each kid either performs a variety act or gives a show-and-tell demonstration. In the third part of the contest, he or she answers a question asked by one of the judges—a question that is designed to show how well the contestant can speak without rehearsal. The judges score each contestant for each part of the contest. When they add up all their scores in private, they announce the winner.

Naturally, you don't have to put on a show that is *exactly* like the ones that have been described in this chapter. Instead of a performance recital, you could put on a fashion show. Instead of a variety show, you could put on a series of science demonstrations. Instead of a one-act play, you could put on a read-aloud play, with the actors reading their dialogue out of books. You can take any one of the basic show ideas and change it around to meet your own group's interests and abilities and needs. The important thing is to decide on the kind of show that provides a part for everyone who wants to be in it—and that allows everyone who does take part in it to have a good time.

2. There's a Job for Everyone!

Whether you're a natural-born "ham" or so shy that you get stage fright when you have to answer the telephone, there's a job that's right for you in putting on a show. That's one of the nicest things about a show—there's always a job that's perfect for anybody who is interested.

Look at all the things that need to be done. Arrangements for a place to hold the show have to be made. The scenery has to be planned and made, and so do the costumes. You might need to have posters made and hung. You may need programs for the audience. You'll probably want ushers to show the audience to their seats. You may need someone to run the sound effects. And, of course you will need performers—people to be in the show. Also, someone has to be in charge of the whole thing, to be sure that all the work gets done and that everyone knows what's going on.

And these are only *some* of the jobs to be done. There are lots more! (Of course, you don't need the same number of people for every show, and some shows have jobs that others don't.) Fortunately, many boys and girls like to do more than one job, so if there are more jobs to go around than there are people, some of the kids can take on more than one job. The opposite problem never comes up—you never have more workers than there are jobs—because there's always something that needs doing.

Let's take a look at all the different jobs.

Producer

The job of producer is probably the most important one in any show. That's because it's the producer's job to make sure that every single task gets done, and that it gets done well and on time. The producer is the head organizer.

It would be impossible to list every single thing that a show producer has to do, because the tasks run all the way from big ones, like being sure that it's all right to hold the play at the time and in the place planned, to little ones, like having a supply of thumbtacks, tape, and straight pins on hand on the day of the show to fix anything at the last minute. In a nutshell, the producer is in charge of everything.

That doesn't mean that the producer single-handedly does all the work. But he or she does know what work needs doing, and then gets someone to do it. In a pinch, the producer may end up doing a job himself or herself, but mostly the producer sees that everyone has a job to do, and every job has someone to do it.

To be a good producer, you need several important qualities. You must be well organized, patient, and willing to accept a lot of responsibility. You must have "stick-to-it-iveness," and be able to get other kids to work without being "bossy" about it. And most of all, you must be willing to work hard.

Director

Just as the producer is the head of the whole show, the director is the head of the performance. It's the director's job to be certain that what takes place onstage is as good as everyone can make it. He or she watches the performers when they rehearse, and makes suggestions about ways in which they can improve their performances.

If the performers are going to do specialty or variety acts that they already do well, the director doesn't get involved in that part of their performance. For example, if a girl who plays the piano is going to play a number, the director wouldn't try to tell her *how to do it*, but might make suggestions about when she is to come on the stage, where she is to come in from, and where she is to go off when she has finished.

In putting on a play or other show involving acting, the director is the one who helps the actors play their parts effectively. He or she may tell them when and where to move during certain moments of the play, or suggest that they try to speak louder, or softer. The director suggests ways in which the actors can help make the play as entertaining as possible.

Putting on a play is a team effort. The director is the one who serves as captain of the team. Just as in sports a team captain encourages the rest of the team to do their best, and gives tips on how they can improve, so a director gives actors encouragement and help, so they will do their best.

A director needs many of the same qualities as a

producer. Even though the audience may never see the director, that person's work is up there on the stage just as much as the work of the performers is.

Stage Manager

The stage manager is the one in charge of the backstage area during the performance. This person must know what is supposed to happen onstage and backstage at every point. If scenery or furniture is to be moved on or off the stage between acts, the stage manager makes sure the moving is done on time and quickly. The stage manager tells the person who is

pulling the curtain when to pull it open, and when to close it. If there is someone running sound effects, the stage manager gives the *cue* (signal) for each sound effect. It is also up to the stage manager to be sure the performers are in their places and ready to begin *before* the show starts. And if some calamity occurs during the performance—if the scenery falls down, or the curtains refuse to close—it's up to the stage manager to cope with the crisis. Fortunately, really terrible disasters don't usually happen, although you're always afraid that one will. But, just in case, it's a good idea if the stage manager is someone who can stay calm during an emergency and solve problems quickly and cleverly. It is also the stage manager's job to make sure that everyone backstage is quiet during the show.

Scene Designer

As you might expect, the scene designer is the person who designs the scenery. Not every show needs scenery. If you're putting on an out-of-doors show or a variety show, you can do without this job completely (though you don't have to).

A scene designer must have imagination, so he or she can provide your show with terrific *sets* (scenery) without even spending any money at all. Scenery serves one of two purposes: either it is purely a decorative background, or it tells the audience something about where the show is taking place. A clever designer can accomplish either of those things using very simple materials.

When scenery is needed just to decorate the play area, as in a recital, for example, the scene designer may do it in a number of simple ways. Autumn leaves might be pinned all over the back curtain or taped to the wall. Bunches of balloons hung from the ceiling could give a festive look. Crepe-paper streamers, artfully twined and draped, would make a plain room instantly look fancy. Painting designs such as flowers, stars, or brightly colored circles of all sizes on large sheets of wrapping paper or corrugated cardboard cut from empty store cartons, and then cutting them out and hanging them about the stage is another simple, effective method of decorating the play area. Or the scene designer might borrow lots of potted plants and arrange them in a pleasing fashion about the stage. These are only a few suggestions. The more imaginative your scene designer, the more likely he or she will be to come up with ideas for making the stage look attractive without spending money.

There are similar methods of designing scenery when you need to tell the audience where a show is taking place. The designer might use just one or two pieces of scenery to set the entire scene. A single tree, painted on the side of a very large carton and then cut out, could be all the scenery needed for a play set in a forest. Or, a table and a few chairs, plus one or two pictures hung on the back wall of the stage, might be enough scenery to suggest a living-room. Another approach might be to cover the back wall of the playing space with large sheets of overlapping newsprint or wrapping paper, and then

to paint on the scene design like a huge mural. Another very simple design idea—one that costs no money and that most audiences seem to enjoy—is simply to use signs to tell the audience about where the play is taking place. A large sign tacked to the wall saying FOREST, a sign hung on a coat-tree saying TREE, and a sign hanging on a barrel saying ROCK may be all the scenery your show needs.

It's the scene designer's job to decide how much scenery is needed, what it is to look like, and how it is to be set up. Choosing for your scene designer someone with artistic imagination is fine, but choosing someone with artistic imagination who is also willing to come up with ideas that won't cost anything is even better!

Head Carpenter

The head carpenter is in charge of building the scenery, and works with the scene designer in figuring out how the designer's ideas can actually be put on the stage. If cardboard cutouts are to be used, for example, the head carpenter figures out a way to make the cutouts stand up by themselves—and then supervises whatever work is needed to make sure the cutouts *do* stand up. If the back wall is to be covered with wrapping paper, the head carpenter supervises the job of putting the paper up. In addition to figuring out how the scenery is to be made and seeing that it *is* made, the head carpenter sees to it that all the work is done under safe conditions. This person is also in charge of taking care of any tools that are used, and making sure that they are returned to their proper owners or safekeeping places at the end of each building session. Anyone chosen for this job should be good at working with tools and enjoy building and making things.

Stage Crew

The stage crew is usually made up of a number of workers. How many depends, to a large extent, on how complicated the scenery is for your show.

The stage crew has three main jobs. Under the direction of the head carpenter they build the scenery. Under the direction of the scene designer they paint it. And, under the direction of the stage manager, they set up and take down the scenery during the show. The more people you have helping to build and paint scenery, the faster the work goes. On the other hand, too many "extra hands" backstage during the show can cause noise and confusion. If the stage crew for building is larger than the crew for "running" the show, usually the producer has to divide the work: the members of one crew will run the show backstage, and the other crew will finish their work during the weeks and days before the show is put on.

Costume Designer

Not every show needs a costume designer, but when one is needed, that person should be imaginative, artistic, and capable of coming up with good ideas that

don't cost money. In almost all ways, a costume designer needs the same qualities as a scene designer, and very often one person is chosen to fill both jobs.

When the performers are going to wear their own clothes, you will probably not need a designer. Sometimes, though, it's nice to have one anyway, to come up with suggestions for extra little touches to change the look of everyday clothes into something special. For example, suppose a group of boys is going to sing, wearing their own clothes. The costume designer might make a bunch of big paper bow-ties or a set of matching crepe-paper vests to make them look more like a group.

When some kind of costumes are needed, as in the case of a play, the work of the costume designer becomes more important. Usually, one or two items can be worn by each performer to suggest who he or she is supposed to be. The costume designer will figure out what those items should look like, and how they can be borrowed or made. Paint, paper, and pins are the costume designer's best friends.

Keep in mind that the word "costumes" includes masks and headdresses. Just as one painted tree can represent a whole forest, the right headdress—a crown for a king, or a pointed paper hat for a wizard, or a stocking cap for a jester or an elf—can be all the costume needed. For animal characters, open-face masks are usually best. By cutting a round hole for the actor's face in one side of a large shopping bag, and then painting the rest of the bag with appropriate decoration, you've provided a quick and easy solution to the problem of costuming anything from a frog to a peacock.

A simple costuming trick is to paint the costume on a large sheet of paper, and then pin it to the actor's shoulders. Another solution is to use signs instead of costumes—a girl wearing a large sign that says QUEEN will be regarded as a Queen by the audience, no matter what clothes she is actually wearing.

Costume Crew

Under the supervision of the costume designer, the costume crew makes whatever is needed. (In cases where items are borrowed, great care must be used to ensure that they are returned in the same condition.) The costume crew may also help the performers get into their outfits on the day of the show, and they will stand by to make any last-minute emergency repairs in costumes. When a show is to be given more than once, it's up to the costume crew to check all costume items at the end of the first performance, and put them neatly away so that they're ready to be used again.

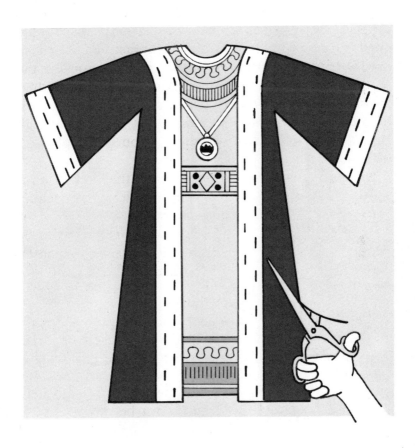

Make-Up Artist

Most girls like to wear make-up, but most boys, even when appearing in a show, dislike it. The simplest solution to this problem is to put make-up on the girls and let the boys go without.

Most shows don't really need make-up, and frequently using it is more trouble than it's worth. It is often impossible to borrow what you need, and buying make-up can be expensive. If the show is given in a place that doesn't have plenty of lavatory space, getting the make-up off the performers after the show can be a problem.

If you feel that make-up is really necessary, the make-up artist is in charge and will help the performers put on their make-up, but only when the performers ask for help. Many people like to put on their own make-up without help, and their wishes should be respected.

Two helpful hints to the make-up artist:

The simplest way to make boys and girls look like old men and women is to dust their hair lightly with ordinary cornstarch, which is perfectly safe and harmless. But before you do it, warn them that they're going to have to shampoo to get the stuff out!

The simplest way to remove make-up from the face is first to cover the face generously with cold cream, and then wipe several times with tissues. Do a thorough follow-up job with soap and water. (There will probably be some make-up traces left, but at least most of it will have been removed.)

Sound Technician

If there are to be any special sound effects in your show, you need someone to be in charge of them—the sound technician. If there are any offstage noises called for—thunder, for example—this person figures out in advance how to create it, and then, during the show itself, makes the noise when the stage manager gives the cue (signal).

Sometimes, it's simplest to record the needed sound effects on tape, and then play the tape recorder during the show. The sound technician does both. Especially when your show requires recorded music, using a tape recorder is the simplest, safest course to follow.

A good sound technician is willing to experiment with sound effects, trying different noises at different levels of sound, over and over, until every needed sound effect is as good and as clear as possible.

Prompter

When performers have to speak memorized lines, there is always a chance that one of the actors will forget his lines. When this happens, the whole show may come to a grinding halt.

A prompter is a person who sits in the wings (the backstage area nearest the stage) with the script of the play in his or her lap. The prompter's eyes should never leave the page, but follow along as the actors speak their parts. If an actor does forget what he is

supposed to say next, the prompter tells him or her the correct words.

Practice is required at prompting, to find just how loudly the prompter must speak. Obviously, the prompter must be loud enough so that the actors onstage can hear. On the other hand, the prompter must not be so loud that the audience can hear. For this reason, prompting can be a tricky business.

It's important for a prompter to go to every rehearsal, in order to learn when there are going to be pauses in the show. For example, an actor in a play is supposed to say "I'm going to my room." The actor then goes to the door, and before leaving the stage adds, "And if Bob comes looking for me, tell him I've gone out." Obviously, while the actor is walking across the stage between those two lines, he will not be saying anything. If the prompter didn't know that was supposed to happen, he might think, during the silence, that the actor had forgotten his lines. He would then whisper the line, "And if Bob comes . . ." to the actor before it was time for that line. While an actor is very glad when a prompter gives him a line he has forgotten, he is usually very upset if prompted unnecessarily. For this reason, a good prompter must be aware of the timing and everything that is supposed to happen during the course of a show.

Curtain Puller

If you are giving your show on a stage with a curtain, you need someone to open and close the curtain. That person is the curtain puller, who takes his cues from the stage manager.

It's up to the director to decide whether the curtains are to open or close quickly or slowly. For example, if a play has a sad ending, the director may feel that a slow-moving curtain would be the best way to close the play. But then for the curtain call, when the actors take their bows, the director might think the curtains should open and then close very quickly. You have to practice working with the ropes that control the curtain to get the knack of pulling them open and closed at the right speed, and in a steady movement. A curtain that jerks open in fits and starts usually makes the audience laugh.

Publicity Director

If you need to interest people in becoming part of the audience for your show, you need a publicity director, whose job is to figure out the best methods of announcing the show in advance, so that people will begin to look forward to it and make plans to attend. The publicity director might decide to put up posters in the area, or perhaps distribute handbills. In some communities, a local newspaper might be willing to run a notice about your show in advance, and it's up to the publicity director to give the newspaper the information it needs.

Usually it takes more than one person to handle the publicity, so the publicity director has to have a committee to help get the work done.

All the publicity for the show must include the name of the show, the date and time it will begin, the place it will be held, and the cost of tickets, if any. If the money

from tickets is going to be used for some special purpose or given to a charity, that should be mentioned in the publicity, too. And if the show is being put on by an organized group, the name of the group should be included.

Program Manager

If you are going to give out programs to the audience, you need a program manager. This person must get all the correct information to include in the program from the producer, and then arrange to have the programs made. For a small audience, programs can be typed or hand printed, using carbon paper to make extra copies. For a large audience, you'll probably want to arrange to have the programs mimeographed or run off on a xerography machine.

Of course, you don't *need* programs for your show. They usually cost money—and they usually create a litter problem when the show is over. If you want, you can have someone come onstage before the show begins and simply *tell* the audience whatever it needs to know.

If you do have a program, it should include the following information:

Name of the group putting on the show;
name of the show;
order of acts in the show;
names of the performers and their rôles;
names of the people doing behind-the-scenes jobs; and
special notes of thanks, mentioning the names of any people or groups in the community who have given special help to you in putting on the show.

Before you make up the program, triple-check to be sure that everybody's name is spelled right!

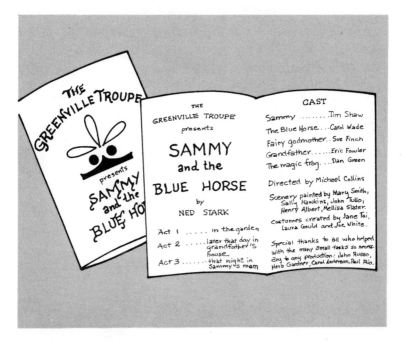

The program reads:

THE GREENVILLE TROUPE
presents
SAMMY and the BLUE HORSE

THE
GREENVILLE TROUPE
presents

SAMMY
and the
BLUE HORSE
by
NED STARK

Act 1 . . . . . . in the garden
Act 2 . . . . . later that day in grandfather's house
Act 3 . . . . that night in Sammy's room

CAST

Sammy . . . . Tim Shaw
The Blue Horse . . . Carol Wade
Fairy godmother . . Sue Finch
Grandfather . . . . . . Eric Fowler
The magic frog . . . Dan Green

Directed by Michael Collins

Scenery painted by Mary Smith, Sally Hawkins, John Tullo, Henry Albert, Mellisa Slater.

Costumes created by Jane Tai, Laura Gould and Joe White.

Special thanks to all who helped with the many small tasks so necessary to any production: John Russo, Herb Gardner, Carol Anderson, Paul Rio.

House Manager

The part of the theatre area where the audience sits—is called "the house." The house manager is in charge of supervising this audience section just before and during the show. The house manager ensures that the house is tidy before the audience comes in, and after they arrive enforces any special rules ("No Food Allowed in the Auditorium"). And, if necessary, the house manager helps maintain order in the audience. Particularly when there are a lot of very little children in the audience, the house manager may have to do a good bit of "shushing" and reminding the little ones to walk, not run. The house manager is also in charge of cleaning up after the show.

Cashier

If you are charging admission to your show, you need a cashier to sit at a table inside the door to sell tickets. The cashier's job is a very responsible one. He or she should be good at arithmetic and very careful about making correct change. It's also up to the cashier to make proper arrangements for the safekeeping of the ticket money, and for the prompt delivery of the money to a responsible person at the end of the show.

Adult Adviser

Even if you and your pals want to put on a show all by yourselves, it's a good idea to have an adult adviser for your show. Sometimes quarrels break out among the best of friends, and it can be helpful to have a grown-up around to help settle things. An adult adviser can also make suggestions when problems arise, and in even the best-planned show, problems sometimes arise. When things begin to go wrong, it's a comforting feeling to know that there's an older person to turn to. (Some adult advisers have been known to take everyone involved in putting on the show out for pizza afterwards —and that's nice, too!)

Other Jobs

For very large shows, you might add these jobs to your list:

Ushers

Ushers help members of the audience find empty seats, and give them programs, if there are any.

Choreographer

If there are to be dances in your show and they need to be newly created, you will have to have a choreographer, who is a designer of dances, and tells the performers, movement by movement, how the dances are to be performed.

Electrician

If there's more to the lighting for your show than the simple turning on and off of light switches, you will need an electrician who is responsible for all show lighting. Because lights and electricity are *very* tricky, and can even be dangerous, this job should *always* be performed by an adult.

Properties Master

Objects handled by actors in a play are known as properties, or, for short, props. (In some shows, furniture used as part of the scenery is also considered part of props; in other shows, it's the scene designer who is in charge of furniture.) If your show involves props, you will need a properties master to round them up in advance, and to take care of them backstage.

Accompanist

If your show involves singers, dancers, jugglers, or other performers who require a musical accompaniment with their act, you need an accompanist. This person usually performs on the piano at one side of the stage.

But if your group has a guitarist, or a banjo player, or a drummer, or a flutist, or another musician, perhaps one of them could be the accompanist. Or perhaps you could have a whole combo serve as accompanists.

Ticket Committee

If tickets are going to be sold before the day of the show, you will need one or more people to take charge of this job. Generally speaking, selling tickets in advance is *not* a good idea, as it is often more trouble than it's worth. But for a really big show, it may be necessary. Make sure that the members of your ticket committee are very careful about keeping accurate records of the tickets they have to sell and the money they receive for tickets sold. The chairperson for this committee would also be the logical person to be in charge of having the tickets printed up.

We said at the beginning of this chapter that there was a job for everyone who wanted one. By now, we think you'll agree. But if there is someone who wants to help who doesn't want to do *any* of the jobs listed, or if all the jobs listed have been filled and there is still someone left over, use your imagination and come up with another job that needs doing:

■ Popcorn seller.
■ Someone to help set up chairs for the audience.
■ Someone to write thank-you notes to everyone who helped in putting on the show.
■ And there's one more possibility, too. Maybe you could use another person to be *in* the show!

3. Variety Shows and Revues

In many ways, the easiest show to put on is either a variety show or a revue. Both consist of many different short acts, one presented after another. They usually require very little scenery, costumes, or make-up. Most individual acts will be acts that the performers have already practiced: a girl or boy taking dancing lessons may do a tap dance, a violin student may play one or two selections, a magician may show tricks already mastered. This means that you won't need a lot of rehearsal time to get your show ready. It also means that the performers can rehearse their parts by themselves or in small groups. Only a few days before the actual show will it be necessary for you to round up all the performers at the same time and in the same place. So, you really ought to consider putting on either a variety show or a revue—especially if this is going to be the first show you have ever put on.

Although there are some differences between a variety show and a revue, they are like one another in many respects, so let's cover both of them at the same time, pointing out differences as needed.

What Talent Is Available?

The first thing is to make a list of the acts that you can count on. If Shirley plans to play a piano selection, write that down. If Lou and Dale want to do a novelty dance, write it down. Are there any magicians, jugglers, instrument players, combos, singers, or dancers you can definitely count on for your show? Add them to your list.

You may discover that you are lucky enough to have plenty of "acts" all ready to make a complete show.

A variety show or revue should last between 20 minutes and 30 minutes, so your show will have time for six or eight separate acts. If you have more than enough kids to fill out the show, it's usually better to add more acts, keeping each one very short, than it is to keep out some kids who want to be in the show. Not only does this prevent hurt feelings, but it also helps build up a larger audience, because each performer is sure to have parents and a few special friends who will come only if he or she is in the show.

In planning the acts, arrange things so that no two similar acts are presented one right after the other. If there are three different kids, for instance, each of whom wants to sing a song in the show, it will be more interesting to the audience if one of them is the first act, one is the fourth act, and one is the sixth act, than it would be if the three songs were presented one right after the other.

What can you do if you only have four acts ready for your show? Do you have to wait until you find two more kids who do special things? No, you don't! You can put together a couple of acts to fill out the program, using kids who don't have any special "thing" of their own. You might call these acts, "Talent Acts for Kids with No Special Talent." Here are some for you to consider:

The World's Worst Anything

This act is actually improved when the performer has no talent whatsoever in the thing being done. Simply announce the act as "The World's Worst Singer" or

"The World's Worst Dancer" or "The World's Worst Magician" or whatever. (Be sure the "worst" act doesn't conflict with an act someone else is doing. If you have no magician, then it's all right to do "The World's Worst Magician," but not otherwise.)

The person is announced, he or she comes out, and, very seriously does the act, but doesn't *try* to be funny. The performer pretends to be very serious and very sincere in performing, and that's what makes the act really funny. The harder the performer tries, and the more difficulty he has, the funnier it is. For example, "The World's Worst Singer" should not only have absolutely no ability at carrying a tune, but also should try to sing a very complicated piece of music, such as an operatic aria.

This kind of act should be kept very short. But it is almost a sure-fire hit with an audience—*and* it's a great way for someone without a special talent to be in the show.

A Record Pantomime

This is another act that requires no special talent and can be put together fairly quickly and easily. A record is played offstage, and the performer moves his or her lips to match the words on the record, pretending to be doing the singing. Two things help this go over really big. First, the performer onstage should use very exaggerated gestures. The wilder the motions, the funnier the act. Second, it should be ridiculous to think that the voice on the record could possibly ever come out of the

mouth of the performer onstage. For example, it's especially funny if a tiny girl does a pantomime to a record sung by a man with a deep bass voice. Or a boy could pantomime a record sung by an operatic soprano.

A successful record pantomime takes a certain amount of practice. You have to memorize not only the words of the song on the record, so that you can move your lips convincingly, but you also have to memorize exactly the rhythm and tempo of the record, so that your lip movements and gestures match the record exactly. But if you're willing to do some rehearsal, you can end up with a terrific act.

If you're willing to do a *lot* of rehearsal in advance, you can make your record pantomime even more elaborate. For example, you could choose a record that has two people singing. You could pantomime both parts, putting on a funny hat when you are pretending to be the first singer and whipping the hat off when you are pretending to be the second singer. Or—and for this, you will need the help of a good sound technician—you could pantomime a record that has a scratch in it, so that you have to keep doing the same words over and over, getting more and more frantic and trying desperately to signal the sound person offstage, until finally the needle on the phonograph is pushed off the scratch so that you can finish the number. Of course, more than one person can do a record pantomime, too, but the more people involved, the more rehearsal will be needed.

The Incredible Swami River

Another act that doesn't take any special talent but does take some practicing is a mind-reading act, which is always popular with audiences, partly because members of the audience get to take part in the act.

To do a swami act (a swami is a wise man in a turban and flowing robes who is supposed to know the answers to all questions), you will need two people. One of them plays the swami, or mind-reader; the other, in the audience, talks to people in the audience and shouts up to the swami on the stage. The partner, of course, is in on the trick, and is the one who makes it possible for the swami to get the right answers.

There are many different methods that have been worked out for mind-reading acts. You will find them described in books of stunts and games that you can find in your library. Here is one to give you an idea of how you can rig an act like this.

The swami comes out onstage and gives a short speech about his or her mystical powers. It should be full of nonsensical mumbo-jumbo. He then announces that he will sit in a chair with his back to the audience and his face covered, but that he will still be able to identify any object held over his head by his assistant. He brings out a tall pointed hat, and demonstrates that when the hat is on his head, it comes far down over his eyes and nose, so that he cannot possibly see. His assistant invites anyone in the audience who cares to examine the hat to do so. When the examination is over, the swami puts on the hat.

The assistant leads the swami to a chair, and seats him with his back to the audience. The assistant then goes down into the audience, and asks people to lend him small objects from their pockets or purse. The assistant takes the objects up onstage. One by one he holds them over the swami's head—and sure enough, the swami announces in loud tones what each object is.

Here's how it's done. The trick is not, as you may think, based on any holes in the swami's hat. Indeed, it is very important the hat be whole, so that it *can* be examined by anyone in the audience who wishes. *But,* when the assistant goes down into the audience, the swami removes from his pocket a small mirror, and holds it in his lap, unseen by the audience. By looking down his nose into the mirror, he will be able to see the objects held over his head. Some advance practice will enable the assistant to know just how high and where the objects must be held to be sure the swami can see them.

Running Gags and Blackout Sketches

Another way to add sparkle and variety to your show, and at the same time to give kids without special talent a chance to perform, is to use what are called running gags and blackout sketches.

RUNNING GAGS are very short dialogues presented between the major "acts." They are really just illustrated jokes, and, in fact, the comic pages are a good place to find ideas. They are called "running" gags because they "run" throughout the show. Usually, all of these short bits are related to one another in some way.

Here's a running gag that only involves one performer, but a lot of props. After the first act, a performer enters at one side of the stage, carrying a tiny plant in a flower pot. He holds the pot on one outstretched hand, and simply walks across the stage with it and off the other side. This usually puzzles the audience, but the show goes right on. After the second act, the performer enters carrying a larger flower pot, with a larger plant in it. Holding it in both hands, he simply walks across the stage and off the other side. After the third act he repeats his "thing," only now the plant is so big he has to use both arms and hands to carry it. Each time, the plant and the pot are bigger, and the performer has to work harder to carry them across the stage. At the very end of the show, the plant and pot are absolutely enormous—and the plant may have burst into flower. The performer has to pull them onstage by a rope tied to a wagon. (The big plants can be artificial.)

This is a very simple running gag, but audiences seem to enjoy it. They actually begin looking forward to the next appearance of the plant, and it has happened in some shows that the gigantic plant got a bigger round of applause than any of the performers.

Running gags with dialogue can be performed between the major acts, too. For example, suppose you decide to do a series of running gags about a rich woman and her funny maid. You need two actresses, one for each part. When the curtains close on the first act, the two could come out from the left side of the stage, and have the following conversation:

Woman: Mary, didn't I tell you to go to the butcher's to see if he has pig's feet?

Maid: Yes, ma'am. And I did just that.

Woman: Well?

Maid: Well, to tell the truth, ma'am, his pants were so long, I couldn't see if he had pig's feet or not.

(Woman gives a wail, and the two go off.)

After the next act has been performed, the two come out again—this time, just for variety, from the right side of the stage.

Maid (angrily): I quit! This job's too much for me!

Woman (surprised): Why, Mary, yesterday when you scrubbed floors all day, you seemed perfectly happy. But today all you've had to do is go over the fresh straw-berries and separate the bad ones from the good ones.

Maid: That's just it, ma'am. I don't mind hard work—but decisions, decisions, decisions all day long are killing me!

(Woman gives a wail, and the two go off.)

After the next act has been performed, the two come out again—maybe from between the central opening of the curtains.

Woman: Mary, there is a terrible smell in this room. Did you change your socks today?

Maid: I sure did, ma'am. And I've got my old ones here to prove it!

(Pulls socks from apron pocket. Woman gives a wail, and the two go off.)

This sort of thing can continue throughout the show. The fact that it is the same two characters taking part in each running gag, and that each little scene ends in the same way, add to the audience's pleasure.

The number of running gags you come up with is limited only by your own imagination—and by the number of joke books there are in your local library.

A BLACKOUT SKETCH is very much like a running gag—except that it is usually longer, and instead of happening several times during the show between the acts, it happens only once and is actually an act in itself. It's

like a very short, very fast, funny one-act play. Often a sketch is no more than several related jokes strung together, usually ending with the most outrageous one. (For example, you could put a number of jokes about silly maids together into one scene, and then you'd have a blackout sketch instead of a series of running gags.) These sketches are called "blackout" sketches because they are often brought to an end by all the lights going out. The "blackout" becomes a sort of super punchline.

Here's a quick and easy blackout sketch that you can rehearse in about a minute and a half:

(Joe is seated at one side of the stage, speaking into a telephone. Jim is seated at the other side of the stage, also speaking into a telephone. They have their backs to each other, and are supposed to be in different places.)

Joe: May I speak with Jim Jackson, please?

Jim: This is Jim Jackson speaking.

Joe: Oh, come on. I'm a friend of Jim's. I know his voice. Your voice isn't the voice of Jim Jackson.

Jim: But that's ridiculous. Of course it's the voice of Jim Jackson. I'm Jim Jackson.

Joe: Are you really Jim Jackson?

Jim (beginning to get irritated): Yes, I'm really Jim Jackson!

Joe: Well, you don't sound like him.

Jim: Well, this is Jim Jackson speaking all right.

Joe: You're sure this is Jim Jackson?

Jim: Yes, I'm sure this is Jim Jackson.

Joe: Well, listen, Jim. This is Joe. I'm in big trouble, and I need to borrow a hundred dollars. (Make this any large amount.)

Jim: All right. I'll give the message to Jim just as soon as he comes in.

(Blackout.)

In addition to making up your own sketches from jokes you find in books or the comic strips, you may find at the library,books that have skits and sketches you can use. Choose one that is *very* short to fit in with the other acts in your variety show.

Themes for a Revue

A revue consists of a number of sketches, mixed with more than a couple of acts, and usually has a theme, while a variety show doesn't.

A theme makes the different elements in your show all hang together. Holiday themes are a good example of this. If you are giving your show at Christmas, you might want to make every part of the show relate to Christmas in some way.

How can you do this? Include Christmas carols, and decorate the stage in red and green, using traditional

Christmas designs. You might also have a performer whose act had nothing to do with Christmas (a magician, say) wear a Santa Claus costume. Your running gags could all be about Christmas shoppers, and someone could give a recitation of *The Night Before Christmas.*

A theme isn't essential, and if you do have one, every single act doesn't have to relate to the theme. But using the theme challenges your imagination, and can help to make the show more enjoyable for the audience. A central theme makes a variety show or revue seem more "all of a piece." Here are some other theme suggestions:

- Mother Goose Land.
- Around the World in Half an Hour (different nationalities).
- My Country, 'Tis of Thee or God Save the Queen (patriotic numbers, spoofs of characters from history).
- That Terrific Rainbow (using a different color as a theme for each act).
- Hooray for Hollywood (doing the whole show as if it were a movie).

Announcing the Acts

If you have typed or printed programs for your show, there is no need to announce each act. They can all be listed in the program, and the show can move quickly along. (Keeping things moving, without any major pauses or waits, is important for a successful show!)

However, programs or no programs, you can still use a performer to announce the acts. This person is known as the *M.C.* (Master of Ceremonies if it's a boy who does the part, and Mistress of Ceremonies if it's a girl). The M.C. comes before the curtains and introduces each act. The announcement may be as short as just the name of the performer and the specialty—"Next, Kenny Kimmons will play *Maleguena* on the xylophone"—or it may be longer, with jokes worked in. If your show has a theme, your M.C. should wear a costume that relates to it.

An alternative way of announcing the acts is to place a large easel at one side of the stage. Before each act, someone comes out and puts on the easel a previously prepared poster that tells the name of the next performer:

This method was used in the days of vaudeville, which was a very popular type of professional variety show.

Whether you decide to do a revue or a variety show, you want to be sure that the performers and audience both have a good time, so keep it bright—keep it fast—and keep it funny.

4. The One-Act Play

When someone says, "Let's put on a show!" most people think of putting on a play. Plays are enjoyable for an audience and a lot of fun for the people who put them on, too. Because there are so many different kinds of plays—comedies, mysteries, fantasies, serious plays—there is sure to be one type that will appeal to your group.

A play is also an immense amount of work. When you and your friends decide to put on a play, you're committing yourselves to spending a lot of time, effort, and elbow grease.

If your one-act play is to be a success, there are two key words to keep in mind: CO-OPERATION and OR-GANIZATION.

Working as a Team

A variety show involves a lot of different people, each doing his or her own thing. A one-act play, on the other hand, involves a lot of different people all working as a team. All of the performers in a play are part of the same act. It isn't enough that each one do his or her own part as well as possible. All must pull together.

Every team has a captain, but putting on a play is so complicated that it needs *two* captains: a producer and a director. The producer is in charge of all the activity related to putting on the play *except* what happens on the stage itself. The director is in charge of what happens *on* the stage.

This doesn't mean that you have two bosses, and everybody else just follows orders. There are many aspects of putting on a play that should be the result of group decisions. Once somebody has accepted an assignment, he or she should be left free to complete it in his or her own way. If Sally has been appointed scene designer, for example, the producer doesn't tell her how to design the scenery. What the producer *does* is make sure that the scenery gets designed, and that if Sally has any problems she gets the help she needs.

Everyone working on the play should try to give ideas, make suggestions, and pitch in and help. But if there are disagreements, the producer or the director should have the last word.

Getting Organized

One of the secrets of a successful show is organizing everything in advance. Knowing all the things that need to be done, and then making a plan to follow will ensure a successful show, on time, and without last-

minute panic. Of course, sometimes something happens that nobody could have expected—the boy playing the leading part gets chicken pox two days before the performance, or a thunderstorm takes down the electric wires in the area where the play is to be held, or some other disaster strikes. If such emergencies happen, just try to cope with them as best you can.

Once the play has been chosen, two sets of plans have to be made up. One is the *production plan*—the list of backstage jobs that need to be done, naming of people to do the jobs, and the making of a time schedule for getting them done. (By reviewing all the jobs listed in Chapter 2, you will be able to write a good production plan.)

The other plan needed is the *performance plan*. This involves the play itself. You must plan a time for try-outs, so that everyone who wants to be in the play has a chance to audition. (The director makes the final decision about who will be in the cast, and what part each actor will play. As many different people as possible should try out for each part, so that the ones finally chosen really are the best choices.) Then you need a rehearsal schedule.

How many rehearsals will the play need before it is polished enough to put on for an audience? How often should you rehearse—three times a week, or every day after school, or every Saturday afternoon? The answer depends, in part, on the actors. As you will need all your actors to come to all the rehearsals, you can only have rehearsals when everyone is available. How long should each rehearsal last? A good rehearsal is long enough to get some work accomplished, but not so long that everyone gets bored or tired or cranky or silly. As most one-act plays are between 15 and 30 minutes in length, a rehearsal that lasts an hour will probably be about right.

After your rehearsal schedule is set, you will have a good idea of when you are going to be ready to put your show on for an audience. While the final choice of a performance date should be made by the producer, everyone working on the show should be involved in the decision. If the director and the actors say they can be ready in two weeks, for instance, but the scene designer says she is going to need more time, her needs should be considered. There's that idea of team-work, again. *Every* person doing a job on the show is important, so everyone's needs must be kept in mind when working out production and performance plans.

Choosing the Play

Probably the single most important decision is choosing the play itself. Here are some of the things you and your friends should think about when deciding on a play.

■ Who will be the audience, and what kinds of plays do they like?

■ How many people are there who want to be in the play? If there are 16 kids who would all like parts, don't choose a play with only a few parts. If there are just a handful of kids interested in being in it, don't pick a play like *The Pied Piper* that needs lots of towns-people and children and rats.

■ Is there a special occasion for performing the play? If it's part of a holiday celebration, for example, or part of some special school or church or Scouting event, you will want to choose a play that is related to the occasion.

■ What are the practical considerations? If you're putting on the play in a playground, for example, there won't be any lighting, so it would probably not be a good idea to choose a play in which someone gets hit on the head when all the lights are out. If your play is in somebody's garage, you might want to think twice about choosing one that needs a piano to be onstage. If you're thinking of a play that needs someone to disappear suddenly, be sure to decide if you will be able to manage it.

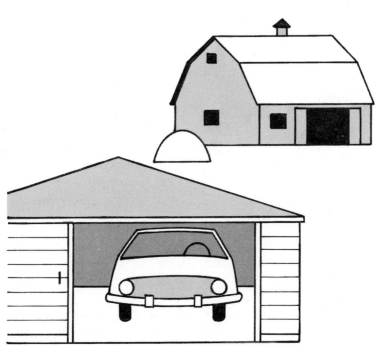

■ How hard do you want to work? Plays that have parts with lots of words mean that you need actors who are willing to do lots of memorizing. Plays that have complicated action—duels, for example, or royal balls—are likely to require many more rehearsals than plays where the characters just sit, stand, walk about, and come in and out of regular doors.

There are many, many books of plays available in the library, and spending some time reading different ones will pay off. The more plays you read, the better your chances of finding just the right one for you.

But putting on a play you find in a book isn't the only solution to the problem of "What play shall we choose?" There's another solution, and in many ways, it's a better one—*write a play of your own.*

Writing your own play has several advantages. First of all, it's fun! Second, it makes it possible for the play to be exactly right for your own group and you can make sure that there is a part for everyone who wants to be in it. If someone in your group has a special talent—like juggling, or tumbling, for instance—you can include it in your play. If there are practical problems facing your group, you can solve them in your play-writing. For instance, if your play is to be produced in a garage, you can write a play whose story takes place in a garage!

Writing Your Own Play

There are several ways to go about writing a play. All of them involve getting a group of friends together to work on the project. The more kids who take part in writing the play, the more good ideas you're likely to get, and the more satisfied everyone is likely to be with the finished product.

You start by asking, "What shall our play be about?" Let everyone come up with as many ideas as possible:

"Let's have a play about witches!"

"Let's do a play about Cinderella!"

"Maybe we could do a play that takes place on a desert island."

"I think our play should have a lot of singing and dancing."

When everyone has made a suggestion or two, it's time to begin discussing the various ideas. Some of the possibilities may be discarded very quickly. Others may create a lot of interest and excitement. Go on talking about each possibility until everyone agrees on one idea. That becomes the starting point for your play. Now the actual writing of the play begins.

As a group, you decide the following questions:

■ What will the story line be? What happens first, what happens next, what happens afterwards? How does the play end?

■ What characters will we need in the play to tell the story?

■ How many scenes will we need in the play? (If you are writing a play based on the story of Cinderella, for instance, you would need a scene in Cinderella's house, and you would need a scene at the Prince's Ball, and then you would need another scene in Cinderella's house when the Prince finds her and puts the glass slipper on her foot.)

■ What words will each character say?

It is when you get to this last step—deciding what each character is actually going to say—that you have several methods to choose from.

One method is to divide the playwriting group into teams, one team for each scene. Each group has the responsibility of writing the dialogue (words) for that scene.

Another method is for the whole group to figure out all the dialogue for the whole play. If you use this method, borrow and use a tape recorder—it will make the job of keeping track of the dialogue everyone agrees to much simpler.

The third method, and certainly the one that is the most fun, is to work out the dialogue for the play through *improvisation*. Improvisation is acting something out on the spur of the moment, making up the words as you go along. Here's how it works:

Suppose, again, that your play is going to be about Cinderella, and everyone agrees that the first thing that should happen in the play is for Cinderella to be bossed around by her stepmother and two ugly stepsisters. Ask for volunteers to improvise those parts. The volunteer actresses then act the scene out, making up the words as they go along.

When they have finished, get four other volunteers to try the same scene. (Or have the same actresses do the scene again, with each one taking a different part the second time around.) Again, let them just make up the words as they go along.

After the scene has been improvised this way two or three times, some very good lines will have been created. Choose what everyone agrees are the best words and lines from each improvisation, and write down the dialogue for the scene. Then, go on to the next scene, and repeat the process.

Not only does this method ensure that the dialogue you end up with is really as good as you can make it, it also ensures that the process of writing the play is not so much work as it is fun!

Premises for Plays

Thinking up the premise for the play is often the most difficult part. The basic idea of a play is called its *premise* (pronounced PREM-iss). Once you have the premise in mind, the rest of the job is fairly easy. Here are some suggestions for obtaining a premise:

ADAPTATIONS

Pick a story that has already been written, and turn it into a play. Plays based on already-written stories are called *adaptations*. There is virtually no end to the stories that would make good one-act plays, and you probably already know a lot of them. There are fairy tales, such as *Sleeping Beauty* and *Rumpelstiltskin*. There are folk tales, like *The Bremen Town Musicians* and *Paul Bunyan and His Blue Ox*. There are myths, like *Pandora's Box*, and legends, like *King Midas and the Golden Touch*. There are historical events that can be dramatized (turned into plays), and there are popular books, like *The Adventures of Tom Sawyer* and *Mary Poppins* and *Winnie-the-Pooh*. And the Bible is full of stories that

would make good plays, like *Noah and the Ark* and *The Journey of the Wise Men* and *Moses in Egypt*.

INTERESTING PEOPLE

You can write a play by starting with an interesting person as your premise. Imagine the stories that could happen if they involved one of the following:

- A woman who looked like an ordinary candy-shop owner, but who was really a witch.
- A little boy who could foretell the future by looking in a secret mirror.
- An astronaut who missed the last spaceship home.
- A man who owned 837 calico cats.
- A girl who never learned how to laugh.

Sometimes thinking about where the play can take place—what the *setting* is—will suggest wonderful story possibilities for you to build on. Consider these strange places as possible premises:

- The inside of a watermelon.
- A gold-mine deep underneath the surface of the earth.
- A deserted one-room schoolhouse, haunted by the ghosts of children of long ago.
- A lighthouse during a terrible storm.
- A valley on the moon.
- The floor of the ocean.

UNUSUAL THINGS

Maybe some curious object will serve as a premise. Think of an ordinary object, and then give it an odd, unusual quality. How about these?

- A typewriter that turns everything into poetry.
- A forest of solid gold toadstools.
- An invisible elephant.
- A piano that plays by itself.
- A grandfather's clock that strikes 13.

Once you have chosen your premise, add two magic words, "What if . . ." Chances are, you will suddenly have more story ideas than you know what to do with.

You can add your "What if?" to the interesting person you've chosen: What if the candy-shop witch turned some of her customers into gingerbread?

You can add it to your strange place: What if the seeds inside the watermelon weren't seeds at all, but were tiny people?

You can add it to your curious thing: What if the magic typewriter made it possible for a poor man to write poems for money, and then suddenly the type-writer broke?

The trick in using the question, "What if . . .?" is to let your imagination run wild. The more unusual the ideas you come up with, the more interesting your play will be.

Now don't stick with one idea. Build on your first idea by adding another to it, and another, and another, and make sure that everyone involved in writing the play adds ideas. To test your imagination and ability to adapt a premise, see "Some Plays You Can Put On," beginning on page 113!

So, go ahead. Pick a premise—nearly any premise will do. Then ask yourself: "What if . . .?"

5. Puppet Shows

If the audience is going to be made up mostly of children younger than you and your friends, it might be a good idea to put on a puppet show. Little kids love puppet shows! A puppet show is also a good choice when the audience is not going to be large.

There are, basically, four kinds of puppets: marionettes, shadow puppets, stick puppets, and hand puppets.

MARIONETTES are dolls with jointed arms, legs, spines, and necks. A string is fastened to each movable part of the marionette. All the strings are tied to a wooden hand-control device. The puppeteer (operator) holds the hand control, and by pulling on the different strings, makes the puppet move. Marionettes are difficult to make, because they need many flexible (movable) joints. And they are tricky to operate, because the marionette strings have a tendency to get all tangled up in one another.

SHADOW PUPPETS are flat dolls, made in sections. Each section—an arm, a leg, another arm, another leg, the body, the head—is covered with transparent paper or fabric. Then the sections are hinged together, and a rod is attached to each movable section. The shadow puppet is held from below, behind a tightly stretched screen of fabric, like sheeting. A strong light is turned on behind the puppet. The light casts a shadow of the puppet on the screen. The audience, on the other side of the screen, sees the puppet's shadow. Shadow puppets are also fairly complicated to make and operate.

Because they are so tricky, marionettes and shadow puppets are really best ignored until you have had some practice making and operating the simpler kinds of puppets. Then, if you find yourself really intrigued with puppetry, you can go on and try your hand at the more complicated types.

STICK PUPPETS, like shadow puppets, are flat, and, like shadow puppets, are operated from underneath the stage area by a puppeteer holding a rod. But there the resemblance between the two ends. Where shadow puppets are complicated, stick puppets are simple. A stick puppet has no separate moving parts, and there is no screen between the puppet and the audience. The audience looks directly at the puppet.

FIST PUPPETS or hand puppets are simple to make and operate. They have hollowed-out heads made of some solid material, and loose, fabric bodies made like sleeves. The puppeteer puts his hand up through the open fabric body of the puppet and slips a finger into the puppet's hollow head. A fist puppet is operated from below. The puppets in old-fashioned Punch and Judy shows are fist puppets.

There are variations on these types of puppets, of course, and you can experiment in making puppets that don't follow any special type exactly. Here, to get you started, are descriptions of how to make simple puppets.

Stick Puppets

Cut out magazine pictures of people, animals, or special characters that you think you would like to turn into puppets. (Advertisements showing pictures of the characters in Walt Disney movies or in T.V. shows for kids may have some great pictures.) Or, better yet, draw your own pictures with crayons, water colors, soft-tip ink markers, or any other way you like.

Paste your cut-out picture onto a piece of heavy cardboard. (The kind that laundries put inside shirts is ideal for this.) Next, carefully cut out the pasted-up picture once again, so that you end up with a picture pasted onto a firm backing.

The final step is to fasten a stick to the back of the picture, so that you can operate your puppet. The stick

should be long enough to reach from half-way down the back of the puppet to about 8 or 10 inches (20 or 25 centimetres) below the puppet picture's bottom edge. You can use wooden measuring sticks or small, sturdy dead twigs of the right length, or wooden paint stirrers. If your puppets are very small, use long pencils.

How big your puppets should be depends on how big a stage area you have. The smaller the stage, the smaller the puppets. (Later in this chapter you will find a discussion of puppet stages and how to make them.) But whatever size you choose, it's important that all of your puppets be more or less the same size as one another, so drawing your own pictures often works out better than using pictures from magazines.

To operate your stick puppet, hold the part of the stick that extends below the puppet's body, and crouching down out of sight, hold the puppet up so that only the puppet can be seen. Then just move the stick back and forth to make the puppet move.

Paper-Bag Puppets

A variation of the stick puppet that is also easy to make and fun to use is a paper-bag puppet. Use the smallest empty paper bag you can find. Fill the bag about half full with torn-up pieces of newspaper. Thrust a stick—the same kind of stick you used to make your stick puppet—into the bag, right into the middle of the torn-up newspaper scraps. Then, with a piece of string or yarn, tie the bag closed around the stick, just at the point where the newspaper scraps stop. When you grab the stick and turn the bag over, it will look something like a big paper lollipop.

Now, put a face on your paper-bag puppet. You can draw on a face with soft-tip ink markers or poster paints, but sometimes these faces are hard to see from a distance. It is often better to cut features—eyes, eyebrows, mouths, moustaches, and the like—out of colored paper and glue them on to the front of the paper-bag face. Or, you can use gummed stars to make the features—four or five stars stuck on, overlapping each other for each eye, a row of curving stars for the mouth, and so on. If you want to add hair, you can staple or tape on strands of string or yarn or crepe paper or anything else you can think of.

Paper-bag puppets are fun even when they have only a head. But if you want to add a suggestion of a body, you can do it by tying a piece of old fabric around the neck of the puppet, so that the fabric hangs down all around the stick, like a skirt. Be sure to keep this skirt-body loose enough so that there will still be room for your hand inside to hold the stick and make the puppet move.

Traditional Fist Puppets

If you want something a little more fancy than a stick or paper-bag puppet, perhaps you will want to try making a traditional fist or hand puppet. (Some people call these puppets glove puppets, but we're saving that name to use a little later in this chapter for a different kind of puppet.) A fist puppet is made in two parts: a hollowed-out head, and a glovelike body.

The best way to make puppet heads is out of *papier mâché*. (That's a French term, meaning "mashed paper." Its correct French pronunciation is PAHP-ee-ay mah-SHAY. Most people say PAY-per mah-SHAY, and as that's simplest, we suggest you say it that way, too.)

First, make a head shape out of a lump of modelling clay. Make it like a ball or an egg. The head shape should be about as long as your middle finger. Model a nose

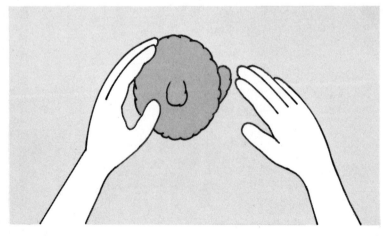

out of clay, and stick it onto the head. If you want your puppet to have ears, model them out of clay and stick them on the head as well. Don't worry about too many details. The main thing is to get a basic head shape modelled.

Next, cut up newspaper (or tear it) into strips or small pieces. Dampen them in water, and then dip them in a bowl of flour-and-water paste. Make sure that the paper gets completely soaked with paste. Then, cover the clay model with overlapping strips of paper. When the head is completely covered, set it aside to dry.

After the first layer of paper is dry, it's time to add a second layer, repeating the steps you used for the first. A puppet head needs to be four to six layers thick. A neat trick is to use regular newspaper for the first layer, colored paper for the second layer, plain paper for the third, colored paper for the fourth, and so on. That way, you can easily tell if you have completely covered the last dry layer with the new wet layer you are adding.

When the puppet head has all its layers and is completely dry, take a sharp knife (it's a good idea to get an adult to help you with this) and *very* carefully slice the head in half lengthwise, cutting from the middle of the neck, up behind the ears, and coming out through the top of the head. Then, before you do anything else, put the knife away in a safe place.

Now, with a spoon, scoop out all the clay from the inside of the puppet head. It doesn't matter if you can't get every last little bit out, but do the best you can.

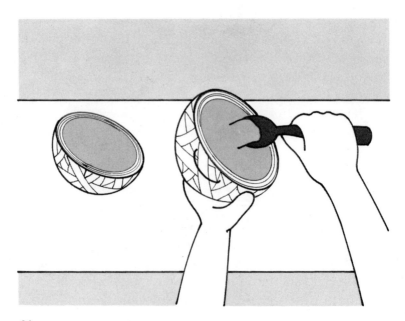

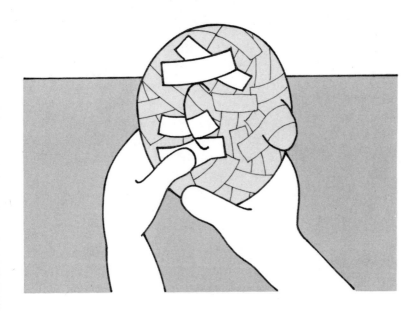

The next step is to fasten the two halves of the hollowed head together. Do this with more papier mâché, and let it dry. Again, use several layers of papier mâché across the cut area to be sure that the final puppet head will be sturdy and strong. Be sure to leave an opening in the neck for one finger!

When the puppet head is dried and in one piece, decorate it. First, paint the whole head with one color of tempera or poster paint, choosing the color that you want as the skin color of the finished puppet. Allow that coat of paint to dry. Then, using different colors, paint on eyes, brows, nose, mouth, cheeks, even warts and beauty marks, if you like! If you are very careful not to let one color of paint touch another, you don't need to let one feature dry before painting the next. But do be careful. Better to go slowly, letting one color dry before starting to use another, than to ruin your puppet by going too fast and too carelessly. You can also add hair, beard, even earrings to your puppets, glueing on anything that strikes your fancy.

Next, make a body for your puppet. You don't *have* to make a body, of course—or you can make a very simple body, like the one described for the paper-bag puppets (page 81). But if you want your fist puppet to be fancy, and if you have a little skill at sewing, you can make a first-rate puppet body without *too* much effort.

Get a pencil and a large piece of plain wrapping paper. (A cut-up brown grocery bag works fine.) Put one hand palm down on the paper, and spread your fingers wide. Trace around your hand with the pencil (holding it in the *other* hand, of course—or you can get someone to trace it for you.) Be sure to extend your tracing down your wrist for about 4 inches (10 centimetres) on each side.

Now, carefully draw curved connecting lines from the base of your pinky (little) finger on the drawing to the base of your middle finger, and from the base of your thumb to the base of your middle finger. Next, erase the drawing of your index finger and your ring finger. The result should be a tracing of your hand with only three fingers. Cut out this tracing. It will be the pattern for the puppet body.

Carefully pin the drawing to a piece of fabric. Lay that fabric on top of another piece of fabric. With scissors, carefully cut around the pattern through both layers of fabric. Pin the two layers of fabric together, and remove

the pattern. Then, either on a sewing machine or by hand, stitch all around the edges, sewing the two pieces together, *except at the place where your wrist was. Leave that bottom edge open!*

Now assemble your puppet. Slip the body over your hand. Poke either your middle finger or your index finger (whichever feels more comfortable) into the middle finger pocket. Put your pinky or your middle finger (again, whichever feels more comfortable) into one of the side finger pockets, and put your thumb into the other. Then, slip the hollowed-out puppet head down over the middle finger pocket. And there you are! By moving your fingers, your puppet comes to life!

Pantry Puppets

Do you want to make puppets in a hurry? You can turn one out in about 5 minutes—if you make it out of a fruit or vegetable. (Just don't try to eat it raw afterwards!)

With an apple corer, hollow out a hole up the middle of a potato, or a green bell pepper, or an apple, or a turnip, or even a chunky carrot.

Use thumbtacks to fasten cut-out paper features to the face of your vegetable.

Put a puppet stick up into the hollowed-out hole.

Tie a loose piece of fabric around the stick at the "neck."

And you've just made a puppet!

Mitten Puppets

Have you lost a mitten? If so, here's how you can turn the one mitten you have left into a puppet.

Carefully sew two big button eyes into the palm of the mitten. With scraps of yarn, embroider a mouth. Be careful that you push the needle in and out of only one layer of the mitten—you need to be able to get your hand inside!

If you like, sew on some scraps of yarn or twine for hair.

Put your hand in the mitten, and the mitten becomes a puppet!

You can make the same kind of puppet out of a mitten-shaped hot-pot-holder. Ask the person in charge of your kitchen to give you an old one that has some burns or tears in it. (The burns and tears will add personality to your puppet.)

If you haven't lost a mitten, and you can't get a hot-pot-holder, you can cut out a mitten shape from two pieces of fabric. Trace a pattern by using your own hand—only this time, keep your fingers together, and just make a U-shaped pattern. Sew the two pieces together, again being sure to leave the wrist end open. There! You have a mitten with no thumb! (If you use this method, you can sew on the features *before* you sew the two pieces of fabric together.)

Glove Puppets

If you have lost a glove instead of a mitten, you can easily make a puppet out of the remaining glove. As with a mitten puppet, use the palm side of the glove for the puppet face. If the glove is made of leather, place features on it with paint, or with cut-up pieces of colored friction tape. If the glove is made of cotton or wool, sew the features on. If you use a floppy white cotton glove—the kind some gardeners and some house-painters wear—make the features with soft-tipped ink markers.

What's really fun about making a glove puppet is figuring out ways to use the glove fingers as part of the puppet design. You could make an American Indian Chief puppet, and the fingers could be his feathers. Or,

your puppet could be one of Santa's reindeer, and the fingers could be the antlers. Or, the fingers could be the antennae of a spooky Martian or other out-of-this-world creature. Or, borrow someone's hair curlers, slip one down over each of the four fingers, and make a puppet lady getting ready for a party.

Another use for a left-over glove is to turn it into the body of a traditional fist puppet. To do this, just cut out the index and ring fingers, and sew up the open places that result. Then, use the glove in the same way as you would a traditional puppet body you made from fabric.

For more ideas on puppet-making materials consult some of the many puppet books at your library.

Stages for Puppets

Whether the puppets you are using are stick puppets, paper-bag puppets, traditional fist puppets, pantry puppets, mitten puppets, or glove puppets, the kind of stage you will need for them is the same. All of these puppets are operated with the puppeteer out of sight, his or her hands held high so that only the puppets are visible.

The simplest way to rig a puppet stage out-of-doors is to throw a blanket, a sheet, or a bedspread over a lowered clothesline, until it reaches the ground. The puppeteers stand behind the sheet, with the audience seated on the other side. Holding up their arms, the puppeteers raise the puppets until they are in view of the audience.

For indoor performances, you can rig the same sort of playing area in a doorway. Hang a curtain or sheet across the doorway, high enough so that it hides the puppeteers standing behind it. Or, the puppeteers could simply kneel behind a couch, and hold their puppets up so that the top of the back of the couch becomes the play area.

Another simple puppet stage is made by turning a table on its side, with the top of the table facing the audience and the legs of the table sticking out into the puppeteers' area. The size of the table is determined by the number of puppeteers. One or two could crouch behind a bridge table; a larger table would be required for more puppeteers.

One advantage of using a table up-ended as your stage is that it allows you to put a "floor" on your stage. To do this, lay a board (leaf from your dining table?)

across the two top legs of the up-ended table. Then put props and furniture on the board, and the puppets can move behind them. You can make the stage even more elaborate by using two boards—one at the front edge of the playing area, one towards the rear. The puppets then move between the two boards, passing behind props and furniture placed on the front board and passing in front of props and furniture placed on the rear board.

However you rig your puppet stage (do keep it as simple as possible) try to set it up so that the puppeteers can either stand or kneel. Those two body positions allow the puppeteer enough freedom to move the puppets easily. A sitting puppeteer or one in a crouch position doesn't have the necessary freedom to make the puppets move easily.

Whether you are using a screen or a blanket or a tipped-over table, you will need lighting for your show (unless it is being held out-of-doors). Lighting is usually most effective when a strong lamp (floor lamps are good for this) is placed at either side of the puppet stage, behind the curtain or screen or whatever it is that hides the puppeteers. If the light comes from in front of the puppets rather than at their sides, too many dark shadows will be cast, making it difficult to see the puppets.

Scenery for Puppet Shows

Fortunately, puppet shows usually don't need elaborate scenery. Most of them can be put on with no scenery at all, but it's nice to have a bit of scenery for decoration.

Because the play area of a puppet stage is so small, you will be able to make scenery easily and quickly out of materials you will probably have lying around the house. The side of an empty corrugated grocery carton may be just the right size for a backdrop. Paint it with poster colors, and tack it or tape it to the wall behind the play area. If there are any unwanted window shades available, and if you are good at simple carpentry, you can rig one of them to work as a backdrop or as a front curtain. If you have two or more window shades, each painted with a different scene, it becomes a simple matter to change scenery in the middle of a play—you just do it with a flick of your wrist!

Another possibility is to use a blackboard or chalkboard for your backdrop. If you have one that is mounted on wheels, move it into position behind your puppet stage and draw your scenery on it with chalk. If your chalkboard is fastened to the walls, see if you can set up your stage in such a way that the board will be in the right position to use.

You might be able to borrow a projection screen to set up behind the play area. Of course, you can't color a projection screen or paint it, but it makes a good, white background against which your puppets will show up beautifully.

Who Speaks for the Puppets?

The simplest way to arrange for puppets to speak is for each puppeteer to say the lines of the puppet he or

she is operating. Puppeteers who operate more than one puppet in a show can change their voices to represent the different characters. When you use this method, a copy of the entire play should be written out in big clear letters, and fastened in a place backstage where the puppeteers can see it easily while they are manipulating their puppets. It's even better if the puppeteers memorize the lines of the play, so they won't have to read at all, but can concentrate their attention on making their puppets move.

Another choice would be to have one set of kids be the puppeteers and another set of kids provide the voices. The second group would have to stand backstage, so that their voices seemed to be coming from the puppets.

This method makes it possible for many more kids to take part in the puppet show—but it also takes extra rehearsal. The speakers have to be completely familiar with what the puppets are going to do, and the puppeteers have to be completely familiar with what the speakers are going to say.

A third possibility is to tape-record the play. Then, at the performance, just switch the recorder on in the PLAY position, and the puppeteers move the puppets around as indicated by the lines on the pre-recorded tape. This method works especially well if you decide to use with your puppets a tape recorded by professional actors of a play for children.

Of course, your puppets don't have to talk at all. Doing a very short puppet show that is simply a lively dance to recorded music can be very entertaining all by itself!

What Should the Puppets Do?

Puppets can put on almost any kind of show that people can. You could put on a play, or a puppet variety show, or a puppet revue, or a puppet concert, or a puppet ballet or even a puppet circus.

If you decide on a play, follow the suggestions in Chapter 3. The same rules that apply to plays with human actors apply to puppet plays. But keep in mind the special quality of the puppet theatre. Things can appear through the "floor" (because a puppet theatre has no floor) as if by magic, and they can disappear the same way. So, especially if you are writing your own play for puppets, try to work into it some special effect that is easy for puppets but that would be difficult for real actors. For example, not only can puppets easily drop into the ground and pop up out of it—they can literally lose their heads!

A puppet show should, as a rule, be shorter than a regular show—the audiences are usually made up of very small children who find it difficult to sit still for long. Also the puppeteers have to work with their arms held up over their heads, and that can get tiring very quickly.

Another general rule for puppet shows is to keep the story simple. A few characters are generally better than many. Three or four simple incidents are generally better than a dozen. Everything about a puppet show should be as simple and as uncluttered as possible.

It's difficult to say who enjoys puppet shows more— the audiences or the people who put the shows on. After you've put on one of your own, chances are you'll decide that it's the puppeteers who have the most fun!

6. When Nobody Wants
to Help

Suppose you want to put on a show and nobody wants to help you. You try coaxing your friends but no matter what you do, the answers are the same:

"Sorry, I'm too busy."

"Naw, I don't feel like it."

"Sounds like too much work."

"Nope, I can't be bothered."

What can you do then?

There are several things you can do. You can give up in disgust, and forget the whole idea. Or—and this is the only practical solution—you can put on a show all by yourself.

Yes, you can!

Of course, it will be a lot of work. But if you really want to put on a show, you shouldn't let the fact that nobody wants to help stand in your way.

Here are some suggestions for different kinds of one-person shows.

The One-Person Specialty

Is there one kind of performing that you particularly enjoy, or that you do particularly well? If there is, use it for *your* show.

If you're an amateur magician, put on a magic show.

If you're a singer, give a recital of four or five songs. (If you are doing it all by yourself, you will either have to accompany yourself on the piano, or you can put the musical accompaniment on a tape-recorder.)

If you're a dancer, give a dance recital. If you enjoy acting, memorize some poems and monologues, and recite them. You can even give a one-person reading, choosing several lively selections from books and reading them to your audience with gestures and emotion, changing your voice for the different characters in the story.

The only two rules you really need to follow in giving a one-person specialty show are these:

1. *Keep it short.* Fifteen minutes would be about as long as your show should be—even shorter, if possible.

2. *Give it variety.* If you're singing, don't choose five songs of the same sort. Instead, start with a short, bouncy song. Then, you might sing a longer, more romantic song. Your third song could be a lively popular tune. Your fourth one could be very dramatic and tragic. And your final song could be one that had a joke at the end of it. There's an old saying among professional show people: "Always leave 'em laughing." That means, end the show in a way that will make the audience laugh, and the audience will know it had a great time.

Similarly, if you're reciting poetry, you could start with something light, like *The King's Breakfast*. Your second selection could be something dramatic, like *Paul Revere's Ride*. And your final selection could be funny—*The Walrus and the Carpenter*. Whatever your specialty, bring variety to it, and you are sure to be a success.

The One-Person Variety Show

If you have a lot of talent and a lot of energy, you can put on a variety show in which you perform all the acts. You don't have to do a first-rate job at all of them, of course. Perhaps you sing well, and you also play the piano well. You could do a five-act variety show by yourself, using those two special talents as the second and fifth acts. Your first could be a record pantomime. Your third act could be The World's Worst Magician (or whatever). And your fourth act could be joke-telling, in which you recite several funny jokes you memorized and worked up into a short routine.

To add to the fun of a one-person variety show, invent strange names for each act (but use your own real name for the last act), and use easel posters showing those names to announce the acts. Also, wear a different get-up for each act. You don't need elaborate costumes— in fact, it would take too long for you to change between acts, and the audience would get restless. But at the very least you could wear a different funny hat for each of your acts. (One act could be performed by "someone" of the opposite sex. If you're a girl, you could do The World's Worst Magician wearing a false moustache and

beard. If you're a boy, you could put on a lady's wig and dress for your record pantomime.)

Just as with the one-person specialty show, it's important that you keep the one-person variety revue short. Remember, you're going to be working very hard, and you don't want to wear yourself down before the show is over!

The One-Person Puppet Show

In any play where no more than two characters are onstage at the same time, a one-person puppet show is possible. The only trick in doing a puppet show all by yourself is to have all of the different puppets lined up backstage in such a way that you can reach them and put them onstage easily. Professionals who do one-person puppet shows solve the problem this way. First, they glue the puppet heads tightly to the puppet bodies. Second, they sew a large metal ring to the bottom front of each puppet body. Then, they fasten a line of hooks into the front or side of the puppet stage. By catching a ring onto a hook and giving a tug, the puppeteer is able to take off a puppet and leave it hanging upside-down in just an instant. It's simple to slip your free hand into the next puppet that is just waiting, hanging upside-down by its hook. It takes a good deal of practice to do this quickly and smoothly, but you can master the skill if you really want to.

Suppose you want to do a puppet show by yourself. Here's how you could do *Little Red Riding Hood* with five puppets.

1. Red Riding Hood and her mother. In this scene, the mother sends Red Riding Hood off to visit Grandma. At end of scene, take off mother puppet and put on wolf puppet.

2. Red Riding Hood and wolf. In this scene, Red Riding Hood explains her errand, and goes off. The wolf tells the audience of his wicked plan. At end of scene, take off Red Riding Hood puppet and put on Grandma puppet.

3. Grandma and the wolf. In this scene, the wolf puts Grandma in the closet and climbs into her bed. There is a knock at the door. Take off the Grandma puppet and put on the Red Riding Hood puppet.

4. Wolf and Red Riding Hood. This is the scene where Red Riding Hood mistakes the wolf for Grandma, and says "What big eyes you have!" and so on. At the end of the scene, the wolf chases Red Riding Hood around and around the room. There is a knock at the door. Quickly the wolf climbs back into bed and Red Riding Hood gets away. Change the Red Riding Hood puppet for the woodsman puppet.

5. Woodsman and wolf. The woodsman sees that the wolf has taken Grandma's place in bed, and he kills the wolf. As the wolf "dies" behind the bed, it is possible for the woodsman to go on talking to the wolf's body while you are actually changing puppets. Take off the wolf puppet and put on Red Riding Hood.

6. Woodsman and Red Riding Hood. Red Riding Hood comes running in and thanks the woodsman for saving her life. The woodsman asks where Grandma is. Red Riding Hood says the wolf must have eaten her. The woodsman says he is sorry, and he leaves, as Red Riding Hood cries. Change woodsman puppet for Grandma.

7. Grandma and Red Riding Hood. Grandma now

comes in from the closet. Red Riding Hood tells her the wolf is dead, and the two are reunited. The End.

Of course, if you *are* going to put on a one-person show, it would be easier if you get one or two people to help you anyway. A helper could announce the one-person specialty, change the signs on the easel for the one-person variety show, and be very useful in assisting the puppeteer to change puppets in the one-person puppet show. There's no reason why you can't have more than one helper and still do a one-person show, and by the same token, there's no reason why you can't do a one-person show without any helpers at all!

7. Some Plays You Can Put On

In this chapter you will find samples of scripts for two plays and one whole play. The first and second are sample plays for puppets, and the third is a whole play for puppets or people and puppets.

You can put these plays on in any way that you wish. You can adapt them and change them to fit the needs of your own group. Or, you can model plays of your own on them, using them for ideas on how plays are written, but writing your own plays instead.

The Princess Who Was Ten Feet Tall

This is a sample of a puppet play using a Narrator—a person who tells most of the story, and who stands at one side of the stage. Standing at the other side of the stage is a girl who plays the Princess Columbine. Between the two is the puppet stage. Except for Princess Columbine, the characters in the play are puppets. This play was written for a puppet stage made by hanging a curtain (or similar drapery) from a clothesline (see page 97).

If you use scenery for the puppet stage, show a room in the king's palace. No special furniture or properties are needed for this play, which makes it very simple to put on. The fact that the Narrator has most of the words, which can be read, also helps make this an easy-to-produce play.

Narrator (At one side of the puppet stage):

Once upon a time, in the Land of Thrall,
There lived a princess ten feet tall.
And oh, how that princess wished she were small!
It was very inconvenient to be such a height.
She had trouble finding dresses that fit just right.
She had trouble not bumping her head against the light.
She was too tall for ponies, she was too tall for sleds,
She was too tall to sleep in ordinary beds,
And she only saw the tops of other people's heads.
But saddest of all, she lived in fear
That a prince to wed her might never appear—
And the fear grew greater, year by year.
Her blood, of course, was Royal Blue,
So only a prince as a mate would do.
But the local princes were just six-foot-two.

(Princess Columbine comes in and stands on the other side of the puppet stage. She looks very unhappy.)

Narrator: Poor Princess Columbine! Life wasn't any fun.
If only *somewhere* beneath the sun
There might be a prince who was ten-foot-one!
As time went by, Columbine grew sadder.

(The king appears on the puppet stage, and crosses over to where Princess Columbine is standing.)

Narrator: Her father, the king, said:

King: What is the matter?

Columbine: Oh Father, dear Father, I lead a wretched life!
   I'll never find a prince who will make me his wife.
(She cries.)

Narrator: Alas, the Princess never even smiled.
   The king, of course, was simply wild,
   For he dearly loved his gigantic child.
   And then—he had an inspiration!
   He issued a Royal Invitation,
   And sent it to every neighboring nation.

King: I hereby issue a Royal Call
   For princes to visit the Land of Thrall
   On Wednesday next to attend a ball.
   My daughter, the Princess Columbine,
   Will stand in the Royal Receiving Line.
   And if a prince proposes—why, that'll be fine!

Now, you and your friends can go ahead and write the rest of the play, using all the ideas and methods you learned on page 68. Remember, this is just the *premise* of your play and you can change it in any way you want.

The Old Woman of the West

This play should be written for a puppet stage that has floorboards (see the discussion on stages for puppets in Chapter 5). The backdrop for the play shows a garden. Growing out of the back stage board is a row of flowers. On the front stage board, at one side, is a large rock. This rock will have to be specially created by your scene designer and head carpenter because it must turn into a fountain!

There are two ways in which you can make the fountain appear. One way is to attach a tassel of shredded cellophane strips to the back of the rock. At the appropriate moment, turn on a small electric fan beneath it. The strips of cellophane will then blow up into view of the audience, producing the "fountain." The other way is to make a stick-puppet fountain: paste a picture of a fountain onto shirt cardboard, cut it out, and fasten a holding stick to it. Then, hold it up at the appropriate moment.

(Without too much trouble, you should be able to figure out ways to arrange your magic effect in such a way that instead of a puppet play, this could become a play for people to perform. Try it and see!)

When the play begins, Nicholas is seen, holding a bucket.

Nicholas (calling): Fritz! Fritz! Where are you, Fritz? *(Shakes his head.)* Is that lazy brother of mine shirking again? *(Calls.)* Fri-i-i-tz!

Fritz (entering slowly): What are you making such a hullaballoo about? It's much too hot a day for all this fuss.

Nicholas: We must work in the garden, Fritz. You know before Mother went away she asked us to take particular care of the garden.

Fritz (unpleasantly): Who are you to order me about? Don't forget that I'm the older brother around here. I give the orders—at least until Mother gets back.

Nicholas: I never saw such a lazybones as you, Fritz. Very well, take your nap—but don't blame me if something bad happens because of your laziness. I must go and fill my bucket at the well, so that I can water the flowers. I have work to do. *(He leaves.)*

(Fritz leans comfortably against one side of the stage. The Old Woman of the West, dressed as a witch, enters slowly from the other side. She stops when she sees Fritz.)

Old Woman: Boy! You there! Boy!

Fritz: Did someone call? *(sees the Old Woman)* Did you call me, old woman?

Old Woman: Yes, boy. It's such a hot afternoon, and I have walked such a long distance. I wonder if you could give me some cool water to drink.

Fritz: I'm sorry, old woman, but there isn't any water here. The nearest water is down at the well, and that's quite a distance from here.

Old Woman: Well, then, would you be kind enough to run to the well and fetch me some water? I've walked such a long distance today. I doubt that my legs would carry me that far.

Fritz (leaning back): Sorry, old woman, but that's too far for me. I'd rather stretch out here and rest in the nice warm sun.

Old Woman: Shame on you, you good-for-nothing lazybones! Don't you know who I am? I am the Old Woman of the West, and many's the magical spell I can weave.

Fritz: Pooh! Nobody believes in magic nowadays. You're just trying to frighten me into thinking that you're a witch, so you can get me to go to the well for you. But I'm not such a fool as that!

Old Woman: You may regret those words, my lazy friend, before the day is done! Mark my words!

(Nicholas comes in carrying a heavy bucket of water.)

Nicholas: Whew, this bucket is heavy! It's hard work carrying it such a distance in the hot sun—but the flowers will be glad of a drink.

Old Woman: Young man, could you spare me a drink of cool water from your bucket? It's such a hot afternoon, and I've walked such a long way.

Nicholas: Certainly, good woman.

(He holds the bucket up and she takes a long drink from it.)

Old Woman: You are a good boy, and a kind one. Not like your lazy brother there! That drink was exactly

what I needed—and it was generous of you to give it to me. You deserve a reward for your kindness, young man, and you shall have it. You see, I am the Old Woman of the West, and many's the magical spell I can weave.

Fritz (disgusted): Are you starting that magic business again, old woman? I've heard enough. I'm going! *(He leaves.)*

Nicholas: You must forgive my brother, Old Woman. He doesn't know any better.

Old Woman: It's not your brother I care about now. It's you—and the reward I promised you. Tell me: is it really a long distance to the well?

Nicholas: It is, rather—but I don't mind. I'm used to going there, for it's my job to fetch water for the flowers.

Old Woman: Very well, then. You will never have to go to the well again.

Nicholas: Not go to the well again? Then how can I fetch water?

Old Woman: Listen! *(She sways back and forth as she recites.)*
Wind from the West, now listen and hear.
Cause a fountain to appear!
Let it gush and gurgle and bubble and swell,
So that Nicholas need never more go to the well!
Presto-pa-desto! Zam!

(She points to the rock, and suddenly a fountain bubbles out of it. At the same moment, the Old Woman drops out of sight.)

Now, what do *you* think happens next? How will Fritz feel when he finds out the old woman *is* a witch?

Carry out the rest of the play by "improvising" as you learned to do in Chapter 4!

The Braggart's Clever Wife

This is a whole play for puppets or actors and *at least one* puppet. Note that it is flexible in the number of people who can take part. If you have very few actors available, you can make all of the parts of the residents of the mountain into puppets. If you have more actors than there are parts, you can divide up the residents' parts and create additional parts that way. And, of course, as many people as you like can take part in the dance at the end of the play. For the part of Magwitch the Giant, use a broom to make a large stick puppet.

The scene is a room in a peasant cottage, which is easy to arrange. The play only needs two entrances (or ways of getting on the stage); at one side is an entrance to the rest of the cottage, and at the other side the entrance leads out-of-doors. The furniture is of the simplest kind—just a table and a few chairs, benches, or stools. Only one costume is absolutely necessary—the long white nightdress and bonnet—and even that doesn't have to be white, and it doesn't have to be a nightdress!

(When the play begins, Miga, the wife, is sitting in a chair, sewing on a long white nightdress. After a moment, her husband, Johnkin, is heard offstage, calling from outside.)

Johnkin (from outside): Miga! Miga! I'm home! Come and let me in!

(Miga puts her sewing down, rises, and goes to the doorway

where she opens the door for her husband—or pretends to, if there isn't a door. Johnkin comes in, carrying a large basket of vegetables.)

Miga: Welcome home, husband! Did you have a good day in the fields?

Johnkin (putting the basket down on the table): Oh, am I tired! How I worked today! You know, Miga, I don't believe anybody in the history of the world has ever worked as hard as I worked today!

Miga (shaking her head and smiling): Now, now, Johnkin. I'm sure you worked hard. But I don't think you worked as hard as all that!

Johnkin: Of course I did! Why, Miga, you don't seem to appreciate that your husband is the hardest worker there ever was. And just look at these vegetables I gathered today. Did you ever see a more beautiful pepper than that? Tell me honestly, Miga, isn't that the most beautiful pepper in the whole wide world? And look at this squash! Surely that is the biggest squash ever raised by a farmer in the whole history of man! And what about this onion? I'll bet that even in the Garden of Eden there wasn't a more perfect onion than this! You've got to admit, wife, that you really married someone special when you married me!

Miga (sewing on the nightgown): Oh, Johnkin, Johnkin, why must you brag so? Isn't it enough that you raise good vegetables? Do they *have* to be the best vegetables in the world? Isn't it enough that you are a good man? Do you *have* to be the best man that ever lived? And even if those things *were* true, it isn't right that you should be the one to say them. It sounds like boasting. It

127

sounds like bragging. And braggarts always get into trouble with all their brag.

Johnkin: I'm not bragging. And I'm not boasting. I just happen to be the greatest man that ever lived, so when I say it, I'm only speaking the simple truth. *(Miga just shakes her head and goes on with her sewing. Johnkin moves towards her, and stands near her, his hands on his hips.)* Who else but the greatest man in the world would have had the courage to build a house right on the top of Magwitch Mountain?

Miga: Hush, Johnkin! You know I don't like you to

speak of Magwitch! You know I don't like you even to mention his name!

Johnkin: Huh! You're as bad as all our friends. They're all afraid of Magwitch, too! But I'm not afraid of him!

Miga: Then perhaps you are a fool. Everyone knows that Magwitch is a strong man. Everyone knows that Magwitch is a mean man. And everyone knows that Magwitch would be very angry if he knew that people had come to live on his mountain.

Johnkin (swaggering around): I don't believe it! That's all just idle gossip! No man is as strong as I am! Besides, nobody has even *seen* Magwitch. I don't even believe there *is* such a person!

Miga: Oh, there is such a person, all right. The only reason we've never seen him is that he is off on the other side of the world, visiting his children. But someday he'll come back. And when he does, there'll be trouble, mark my words. He won't like it that you built this house on top of his own personal, private mountain. He won't like it that you encouraged others to build houses on his mountain, either. You ought to be grateful that Magwitch *is* on the other side of the world, and not go swaggering and braggering about!

Johnkin (crossly): Oh, don't go on and on about it, Miga. I can take care of myself. I'd like to see Magwitch try something on me, that's all. He'd soon find out who was the strongest man in the world!

Miga: I hope you never have occasion to meet him, that's all I can say!

Johnkin: Enough of this foolish talk. Where's my supper? I'm hungry!

Miga: It's just finishing getting cooked in the oven. As soon as I am done sewing the hem on this nightgown of mine, it will be ready.

Johnkin: I hope you have cooked a fine supper for me, Miga! After all, I am the greatest man in the world, and I deserve the best!

(There is a knock at the door—or offstage at the side where the door is supposed to be.)

Miga: Why, who do you suppose that can be?

Johnkin: I will go and see. *(He opens the door and admits a group of neighbors. They all are very excited about*

something.) Welcome, neighbors, welcome! Come in, come in!

Derf: Oh, Neighbor Johnkin, have you heard the news?

Lardo: I knew something terrible would happen—I always knew it. And now it *has* happened!

Groll: What is to become of us? What is to become of us?

Tyl: We never should have come to live on this mountain! We never should have done it!

Johnkin: What news are you talking about? Why are you all so excited?

Derf: You mean you and Miga have heard nothing?

Miga and Johnkin (together): Nothing!

Derf: Tell them, Tyl.

Tyl: Not I! Groll was the one who heard the news first. Let Groll tell it!

Groll: No, no, I'm too nervous. You tell them, Lardo.

Lardo: No, Derf is the best speaker. I think Derf should tell.

Miga: Well, I wish *someone* would tell us the news— and do it quickly!

Derf (nervously): Well . . . the fact is . . . Magwitch has come back!

Miga: No!

Lardo: Yes! His coach was seen in the village this morning!

Groll: He was seen at the inn having lunch this noon!

Tyl: And he . . . he has been seen on his way up the mountain. Not more than 15 minutes ago!

Miga: Are you sure?

Neighbors (together): Yes, we're sure!

Groll: Oh, Johnkin, what are we to do? When he finds out we all built houses on his mountain without his permission, he . . . he will probably do something dreadful to us!

Lardo: You've got to help us, Johnkin! You've got to save us from Magwitch!

Johnkin (who has been very frightened ever since he heard the news): M-m-m-me? D-d-d-do something about M-M-M-M-Magwitch?

Lardo: Yes! The rest of us are just ordinary men and women. But you're always telling us you're the strongest man in the world! Surely if anyone can help us, it is you.

Tyl: And after all, Johnkin, the only reason the rest of us built houses on Magwitch Mountain was because you said it was all right for us to.

Derf: That's right, Johnkin. You said we were all simpletons and sillies to be afraid of Magwitch! You said that no such person as Magwitch even existed! And you promised us that if any trouble ever did happen, you would take care of us, because you were the strongest man in the world!

Groll: You *are* the strongest man in the world, aren't you, Johnkin? You can take on Magwitch any old day, can't you?

(Everyone is standing around Johnkin hopefully, expecting him to help them. Suddenly he bursts into loud crying.)

Johnkin: Wahhhhhhh! I never meant for you to believe me! I didn't know Magwitch would ever come back!

Derf (amazed): You mean you're *not* the strongest man in the world?

Johnkin (still crying): Of course I'm not. I'm just an ordinary person like the rest of you.

Miga (angrily): Now you see what your bragging has brought us to, Johnkin!

Johnkin (sniffing): Maybe . . . maybe Magwitch won't come up here after all.

(From offstage there is a loud, loud banging noise—as though someone very strong were knocking on the door.)

Lardo (squealing): Ooooh! There he is!

Derf (wailing): What's to become of us?

Groll: Who will save us now?

Miga: I will save you, my friends.

Groll: You?

Miga: Yes!

Johnkin: But h-h-how can y-y-you save us, when we can't save ourselves?

Miga: Never mind how I shall do it—but mark my words, I shall do it!

(The loud knocking is heard at the door.)

Miga: Quickly! All of you! Go into the other room— and be as quiet as mice! Magwitch mustn't know you are here!

(All start out. Johnkin turns in the doorway.)

Johnkin: Oh, Miga, I never realized what a brave woman you are.

Miga: Never mind about that! *(She hands him the nightgown.)* Put on this nightgown, and the bonnet you will find hanging by the bed.

Johnkin (outraged): What? You want me to put on a woman's nightgown and bonnet? Why, I'll be the laughingstock of all our neighbors. I won't do it!

(The knocking is heard again.)

Miga: Do you want to be saved from Magwitch?

Johnkin: Yes, yes, yes!

Miga: Then do as I say. Now go! Quickly!

(She pushes Johnkin off into the inside room. Then she crosses her fingers for luck, and takes a deep breath. Finally, she goes and opens the door. Magwitch comes in. He must be much bigger and stronger looking than anyone in the play. He speaks very loudly and angrily.)

Magwitch: What took you so long to open the door, woman? I pounded and pounded on it, but still you didn't come.

Miga (sweetly): I heard no knocking, sir.

Magwitch: What? After all that pounding, you heard nothing?

Miga: Well, sir, I will tell you why that is. You see, my husband is a giant. And I am so used to the noises that *he* makes, any noises that are smaller, why, I just don't hear them at all.

Magwitch (confused): You say your husband is a giant? But I thought your husband was Johnkin.

Miga: Oh yes, Johnkin is my husband's name.

Magwitch: But they said in the village that Johnkin was just a pipsqueak of a man!

Miga: Oh no, sir. Johnkin is a giant, I assure you. Why, everyone knows that he is the strongest man in the world. But I am forgetting my manners. Won't you sit down, sir?

Magwitch (angrily): No, I won't sit down. I'm here on business. I want to see Johnkin.

Miga: I'm sorry, sir. He isn't here right now. But he should be coming home soon, and you are certainly welcome to wait. If you don't mind, I will just get on with my work. *(She goes to the table and picks up the basket of vegetables.)*

Magwitch: Where did those beautiful vegetables come from?

Miga: Why, these are from our garden, sir. But surely you are joking when you say they are beautiful.

Why, I was just going to take them out and feed them to the pigs.

Magwitch: Feed such beautiful vegetables to the pigs? You must be mad!

Miga: Oh no, sir. I *must* get them out of the house before Johnkin comes home. You see, Johnkin is very particular. He insists that he only be given decent-looking vegetables. Why, if he ever saw such puny, ugly, little vegetables as these, he would become very angry.

Magwitch: He must be some fellow, this Johnkin, if beautiful vegetables such as these are not good enough for him!

Miga: Well, sir, it's because of his magical powers.

Magwitch: His magical powers?

Miga: Yes! He just goes out into the garden and says a few magic words—and then we have peppers the size of pumpkins, squash the size of hazel bushes, and onions the size of the moon!

Magwitch (beginning to get nervous): He . . . he really is a magician, then?

Miga: Oh yes, sir. Of course, *most* of the time he uses his magic on people, not on vegetables.

Magwitch: He does? What sort of things does he do?

Miga: Well, sir, it depends. The other day, he became annoyed with one of our neighbors. The man dropped a pebble, by accident, on our front walk. So Johnkin turned him into a toadstool.

Magwitch: For a little thing like dropping a pebble, he turned him into a toadstool?

Miga: That was because he was only annoyed. It's much worse when he gets really angry.

Magwitch: What—what does he do when he gets really angry?

Miga: Oh, different things. Once he worked a spell against a dairyman who sold him some sour milk. The dairyman had to walk on his hands all the rest of his life. Another time, Johnkin became angry at a little boy who who was stealing apples. So he worked his magic, and the little boy became an old man overnight. You know, it's amazing to me that Johnkin can even think up such horrible punishments. But he's as clever as he is strong, so I guess he doesn't have any trouble.

Magwitch: What . . . what do you think he would do to someone who came and said that Johnkin would have to move his house off the mountain?

Miga: Oh, sir, I can't believe anyone would be so foolish as to do a thing like that. Johnkin likes living on this mountain—and he likes to have all his friends living on this mountain, too. Oh, I think he would be very, very, *very* angry at anyone who tried to make him move. I think he would work a *terrible* spell on such a person!

Magwitch: Like . . . like what?

Miga: Well, he might make that person live out the rest of his days at the bottom of a well. Or he might turn that person into a tree—the kind of tree that people like to carve their initials on. Or maybe he'd even cause that person to turn into a puddle of rain water—one that just would slowly evaporate away.

Magwitch: That's the most ridiculous thing I ever heard of! I think you're trying to trick me, woman! Johnkin is just an ordinary man, and I'm going to wait here until he comes home. I have some business with him—and it's business that I don't think he's going to like!

Miga: Well, sir, you may do as you like. I can assure you that Johnkin is a giant, and the strongest man in the world, and one with terrible magical powers to boot. But if you're foolish enough to want to stay until he gets home, why then it's no affair of mine. But if you will excuse me, I must go and get my baby, for it's time for me to give him supper.

Magwitch: So this wonderful giant Johnkin is a father, eh? If the father is all you say, the baby must be pretty wonderful, too!

Miga: Let me bring him out here, sir, and then you can see for yourself. *(She starts for the inner door, then turns back.)* Of course, you mustn't expect too much, sir. The baby is only three days old.

(She goes off into the inner room. Magwitch shakes his head. Suddenly we hear a loud cry in Johnkin's voice from offstage: "Goo, goo, goo!")

Miga (coming back into the room): Here is the baby, sir. *(Johnkin, dressed in the long white nightgown and a baby's bonnet, comes skipping into the room. He makes all sorts of baby noises in his man's voice, and does several athletic stunts—leaping onto the table, picking up a chair in one hand, and so on.)*

Magwitch (amazed): This is Johnkin's baby?

Miga: Yes, sir.

Magwitch: And you say he is only three days old?

Miga: Yes, sir. I'm sorry he isn't a more impressive child, sir, but you see, he's been a little sickly since he was born.

Magwitch: Good Heavens! If this is the baby, then all I can say is, I'm not waiting around to meet the father!

Miga: Shall I tell Johnkin you were here looking for him, sir?

Magwitch: No, no, no! Just tell him this. Tell him Mr. Magwitch happened to be in the neighborhood, and just stopped by to pay his respects.

Miga: I will tell him, sir. Will you, perhaps, come back tomorrow?

Magwitch: No! Unfortunately, I must go back to the other side of the world right away. In fact, I think I will *stay* on the other side of the world for the rest of my life. So you might tell Johnkin that Mr. Magwitch is very happy he likes living on Magwitch Mountain—and that he and his neighbors are welcome to live here for ever and ever and ever!

(During this last speech, Johnkin, still pretending to be an overgrown baby, has been chasing Magwitch around the room. When he finishes his speech, Magwitch runs out, and we hear a loud door-slam.)

Miga: Well, Johnkin, I think we have seen the last of Mr. Magwitch!

(The neighbors come running in, happily.)

Tyl: You saved us, Miga! You saved us!

Groll: Hurrah for clever Miga!

Derf: It was all your quick thinking and quicker tongue, Miga, that solved the problem!

Johnkin (loudly): Hey! What do you all mean? Miga didn't save you. *I* saved you! If it weren't for my clever acting, Mr. Magwitch would be here still. After all, I'm here to protect you. And I'm the strongest man in the whole wide world.

Miga: Oh, husband, will you never stop bragging about yourself?

Johnkin: You are right, Miga. I *shouldn't* brag about myself. But after all, didn't I marry the cleverest woman in the whole wide world?

(Everyone laughs as music is heard. All do a sprightly peasant dance, and the play ends.)

Now, one final word—remember, you and your friends are not professionals, and if your show doesn't come out like a Broadway hit, it doesn't matter one single bit. What does matter is that you—every last one of you from producer to curtain puller—enjoy yourselves putting on the show. And, of course, it helps a lot if the audience has fun, too, and you can be sure they will if you all do the best you can. And that's what this book is all about—to show you that *you can put on a show!*

Index

144